The Smoke of You

A Memoir of Love
During & After Deployment

by

Amber Jensen

MILSPEAK BOOKS
An Imprint of MilSpeak Foundation, Inc.

Manufactured in the United States of America
Library of Congress Cataloging-in-Publication Data
Jensen, Amber
Library of Congress Control Number: 2022943489
ISBN 979-8-9857941-8-2 (paperback)
ISBN 979-8-9857941-9-9 (epub)

Editing by: Ann Wicker
Cover art and design: Michelle Bradford Art

MilSpeak Foundation, Inc.
5097 York Martin Road
Liberty, NC 27298
www.MilSpeakFoundation.org

For Blake—
thank you for understanding that you married a writer,
for encouraging me to tell my version of our story,
and for reminding me to take off my shoes.

One

WHEN I STEPPED OUT OF MY PARENT'S GARAGE, I pretended not to know where I was going. A sensor over the door detected my movement, flooding me in a circle of light. I hesitated but hurried toward Main Street, refusing to interrogate myself.

At the curb, I paused in the glow of street light filtered through maple leaves, then hurried past a memory: Blake and I perched on the hood of my teal Grand Prix on the Fourth of July six years earlier, sneaking away from the street dance for shots of the orange flavored Mezcal I'd brought home from my study abroad in Mexico; Blake shooting the worm at the end of the night; the soapy smell of his white T-shirt as I laughed and leaned in to him.

I walked on, past the single-screen movie theater. Had I lingered there, studied that week's movie poster, I might have pictured Blake, who had worked there all through high school and college, smiling through the ticket window or standing tall behind the concessions counter. I might have remembered myself the summer before my senior year of college, walking up and down Main Street with my new dog, Buckwheat, knowing that Blake would be unable to resist a Labrador and would eventually step out from the theater to say hi. But I brushed past those memories, too, heading south, past the fertilizer plant and my Grandma Betty's old house, in the general direction of the baseball field.

I told myself it was a logical destination. It was my first day back in Bryant after four years of teaching English in Mexico. It was the Sunday of Memorial Day weekend. Our small South Dakota town was quiet, as usual, the weather cool and still, perfect for baseball. The amateur team always played on Sundays, and though I hadn't noticed lights when we drove into town, I knew that if there had been a game, the players would be rehashing each error and hit over a couple cases of Old Mil Light. I also knew that one of those players would be Blake. What I refused to acknowledge was the fact that my only other friend on the team—Blake's older brother, Brock—was at the time deployed to Iraq, and the rest of my baseball friends had either retired from the game or moved to other amateur teams. I lied to myself, imagining that I was walking toward a circle of friends, refusing to admit that I was zeroing in on a single target. But then, the baseball field still two blocks away, I heard Blake laugh.

My pulse quickened.

I recognized the percussive staccato—slightly higher, slightly faster than Blake's usual deep chuckle—indicating that he'd slipped beyond just a couple beers to a little bit drunk. Unable to deny that Blake was the magnet that drew me to the field, I froze, acknowledging the fact that if I kept walking, I was walking toward Blake.

GRAVEL SLIPPED BENEATH MY FEET as I stepped into the dugout.

Several players in green Bucs jerseys turned toward the sound. Conversations paused, open mouths hovered on the lips of cans, as people squinted to make out a new face in the dark. "Who is that?" asked a stubbled, round face.

"Amber," I answered hesitantly.

The face puzzled, "Brittney-Spears-look-alike-contest-winner Amber? Amber Hanson?"

I shook my head and laughed uncomfortably. "No, plain old Amber."

Just as I began to worry that I'd made a mistake, that maybe it wasn't Blake's laugh I'd heard, I recognized his lean frame, angling toward me. "Amber?" His voice raised in a question, his long arms reached for me, the answer to that question. "Is that really you?" He pulled me into an unexpected hug. "I didn't know you were home."

I slipped my hands, which had been tucked into my pockets, out from the pinched hug, sliding them around Blake's back. With a quick squeeze, I laughed. "Just got here today." He held me so tight that I laughed again, patting his back as I confirmed, "So, yeah, I'm home."

Without letting go, Blake leaned back to look me in the eye. "Wait, for good?" He crouched slightly and angled his face down, peering over the rim of glasses he wasn't wearing. "You mean you're staying?"

The smile wrinkles at the corners of his eyes softened me, and I relaxed into his sturdy frame. Before I could stutter an answer, a red-headed kid lifted his baseball cap, scratching his head and walking toward us, jeering, "Jensen, who's the girl? You act like she's the love of your life or something."

"It's Amber," Blake said, jostling me, as if rattling a present to guess what might be inside. "I can't believe you're here." His head bobbed side to side. "We beat Castlewood tonight—and we never beat Castlewood—and now you're here. What are the odds?" He turned, one hand cupping my elbow, the other reaching into a cooler beside him. He shook droplets of water off a silver can, handed it to me, and led me to a bench in the dugout where we assumed familiar positions—bodies turned into one another, knees brushing as we talked, shoulders glancing as we laughed.

We'd spent years flirting in that dugout. Years, drawn together, friends asking what was going on between us, me answering, "Nothing, we're just friends." But I'd always believed there was something more. On that Fourth of July evening six years earlier, after Blake shot the worm, we'd made our way to this baseball field. We'd stood under a cottonwood in the parking lot, and I'd asked Blake why we didn't just go for it, give *us* a chance. He'd answered, "Because you're Amber. You're Win Noem's daughter. Betty's granddaughter. You're smart and beautiful and you've gone to Mexico. You've done things. And I'm just . . . "

I'd objected, pointing out that he was smart and cute and had done things, too. He'd joined the Army, made a commitment to serve his country. But he responded, "Look, I just . . . I know I'd fuck it up if I tried." And although hypothetically I won the argument, pointing out that he was clearly fucking it up by not trying, too, and we'd kissed under that cottonwood tree that night, in the end, he was right. He did fuck it up. Or *we* did. Our attempt at dating was awkward, at best, didn't last long, and I'd moved to Mexico. But now that I was home, the shy boy I'd been trying to love for years wasn't shy anymore. We sat in the dugout that night, falling easily into comfortable conversation, sharing baseball and hunting and family stories we'd told twenty times before, and soon Blake was confessing to me how he'd spent those years figuring himself out.

"I used to worry about stuff, about not doing things right. In college, I couldn't even pick up the phone to order a pizza, sometimes, so you can imagine why I couldn't call you."

"I had no idea," I said. "I mean, I just thought you were shy."

He shrugged, his T-shirt tickling my bare shoulder as he explained. "Shy. Or kind of an idiot. Maybe both." He twisted his neck to look at me. "But I've kind of figured myself out. It's like,

'Blake, you can't let this ruin your life.'"

I sensed the change, not just in words and posture—this wasn't just Blake, emboldened by a couple of beers. It was the change I'd always hoped for, and yet, now that Blake was actively assuming the role of suitor, I resisted. I shifted away from him, planting my hand on the bench between us, stiffening my arm into a barrier. "You know I'm supposed to be getting married, right?" My words betrayed me. *Supposed to.* I softened again, leaning just close enough that our shoulders kissed. "Ernesto's finishing his school in Mexico, he's supposed to be moving to South Dakota next year."

Blake didn't hesitate. "If that makes you happy, that's great," he said. "It really is. I've met Ernesto. He's great. But I don't see a ring on your finger, and you're not married, yet. All I'm asking for is a chance." He stood, pacing in front of me as if presenting closing arguments to a jury. "So, my cousin's getting married next weekend, and then I leave for two weeks of Army summer camp. Will you come with me to the wedding?" Blake extended his hands, pulled me up into a hug.

I nodded my acceptance, "Yeah, I'll go to the wedding."

THE NEXT MORNING, I did a very South Dakota thing. I went for a drive.

Unlike the ambling drives I'd taken with my dad, checking the progress of corn and bean fields, following storm clouds, or the driving around Blake and I had done with his brother on summer nights, listening to music and sipping Old Mil Light, and unlike the destination driving South Dakotans measure in time rather than miles—two hours to Milbank for a baseball game, an hour and a half to Sioux Falls for shopping—this time I knew where I was going but not exactly how to get there. I was going to visit Grandma Betty's grave. I didn't know the name of the cemetery or exactly where to find it, but I had an idea. I followed my instincts.

Heading east out of Bryant, I passed the Lutheran church I'd attended all my life and, just beyond the edge of town on the other side of the highway, its corresponding cemetery, surrounded by a single row of evergreens. I knew Grandma wasn't buried within the shelter of those trees, but they reminded me what I was looking for—the box of evergreens that surrounded most cemeteries. Following some whisper of memory from Grandpa Cliff's funeral when I was a toddler, trusting the gridded ribbons of road I'd been traveling all my life, I drove, scanning the horizon to my left, looking for clues that would lead me.

Three miles east of town, I felt myself swallowed up by the thick grove of trees that, for most of my life, had signaled I was almost home. I slowed out of habit but resisted the muscle memory that would have me turn toward the dairy barn, the windmill, the split-level house where I grew up. I had a feeling the cemetery lay to the north, but as I passed through the trees, recognizing Dean and Marilyn Anderson's beautifully manicured acreage, then the Garfield church another mile ahead—its steeple and pine-lined cemetery an unmistakable landmark—I started to doubt. Beyond the Garfield church lay the road to my uncle Al's farm, Kangas flats, and the Apostolic church. I must have missed something. I thought I knew what I was looking for, thought I could trust myself in this place, but this didn't feel right.

As I searched for an approach where I could pull in, get my bearings, turn around, I spotted a narrow gravel road. I couldn't picture where it would take me, but it presented a possibility. Uncertain, I slowed, turned, coasted forward. Passing an unfamiliar farm place, I began to feel lost, considered turning back. But then sunlight reflected off something silver in the distance: a silver fence, hidden beneath branches.

I parked near a silver archway reading SCANDINAVIAN. Approaching the entrance, I scanned sparse tombstones, certain now that I was in the right place. Leaves fluttered overhead, birds sang, and cicadas squealed as I let myself in. Grandma's grave was easy to spot, the earth in front of it freshly turned.

As I approached the simple grave marker, my instinct was to apologize, "Grandma, I'm sorry I missed the funeral," but that wasn't right. She'd died just two weeks before I was scheduled to fly home, and although I tried to change my plane ticket, I realized I couldn't afford it. But I knew Grandma wouldn't mind. She'd always been satisfied with what she had, never worried about what she didn't, and the memory of our sleepovers, complete with homemade hamburger pizza and freezer-burned pudding pops, meant more than my presence at her funeral ever could. I sat on freshly mowed grass and said, instead, "Grandma, I'm home."

I wrapped my arms around my ribcage, remembered Grandma's lopsided hugs—one breast firm and prosthetic, the other fleshy and soft—uneven like the shuffling limp she developed after hip surgery. "I wish you were still here." As tears welled in my eyes, I glanced to Grandpa Cliff's grave marker. "I miss you, too," I said, remembering the rise and fall of his chest, the buckles of his overalls cool against my cheek, his muffled heartbeat a metronome against which I measured my breaths as I slept. I remembered his armchair, tucked in the corner beside the fireplace at Grandma's, then later living on in the TV room in our basement, my mom patching its green vinyl for years before finally, someone decided it was time to move on. There in the cemetery, I noted the difference between my memories of Grandpa—something I couldn't forget but couldn't quite remember, either, like a phantom limb—and my memories of Grandma, still immediate, the pain of her absence still intense.

I'd seen her five months earlier, just after Christmas. When

I talked to her, then, she fluttered her eyes, as if waking from a deep sleep, and her thick-knuckled fingers fumbled over the back of my hand, but when we perched my niece, Cami, on her lap, Grandma came to life, toddler energy drawing her wrinkled, papery lids wide, her thin lips into a gasp. "Oh, my stars," Grandma cooed. "Look at you." Energized, she'd turned to me and slipped in her usual question: "I suppose you've seen the Jensen boys while you're home?" I tried not to blush. "Such nice boys," Grandma reminded me. "Always bringing me walleye and perch." Blake was the fisherman in the Jensen family, and although Grandma had never seen Blake and I together—couldn't know how we were drawn to each other, how we separated ourselves from others at every opportunity, laughing alone together in the corner at parties or discussing books in the dugout after ballgames—she seemed to envision us together. It reminded me of a story my Grandma Evie, my mom's mom, liked to tell about Grandpa Baine pointing out a group of gangly boys at a high school basketball game in the sixties. "You see those boys?" he'd asked, pointing to the siblings from the rival Bryant Scotties basketball team. "They're Betty's boys. They're nice boys." His comment was cemented in family legacy as a proclamation when two of those boys—my dad and my uncle, Harley—married two of their girls—my mom and her sister, Mary. But now that I needed to examine Grandma Betty's proclamation of Blake as a *nice boy*, now that I sat, poised to test her prediction, questioning whether or not I should give in to what pulled Blake and I together, she was gone.

I plucked a tall blade of crab grass close to the tombstone that read NOEM, wound and unwound the cool green ribbon, then split it into two thin slivers. The smell reminded me of Grandma's farm, of breaking apart milkweed fibers, of splicing Hollyhock bulbs with open blossoms to form faceless dolls. I remembered dizzying spins on the tire swing and rolling down steep ditches, my cousins and I collecting in piles of laughter at the bottom. The memories prompted words. "Grandma, I'm sorry I was gone so long. I mean, it was good for me, and I'm glad I left for a while, because I think I'm realizing something, now that I'm home."

I imagined freezers full of sweet corn. A house messy with signs of life. I tugged at another tall blade of grass that had escaped the mower's blade, pulled it through my fingertips, stripping the seeds that narrowed to an arrow's tip at the top, then let them fly. "I want a simple life. A centered life. The life that you modeled. So, thank you, Grandma, for teaching me that." I stood, letting the sun warm my shoulders, listening to the whistle of birds, the buzz of insects, the whisper of leaves. Before leaving, I added, "And you were right. Those Jensen boys are nice boys."

AFTER TEN YEARS OF NEVER-QUITE-DATING, Blake and I were finally together, our relationship launching into high-speed like spinning tires finally finding a surface to grip. Blake was with me one night at my parents' house when Ernesto called. While I paced, my tongue trilling and gestures flailing as I explained in Spanish that it was over, that he wouldn't be moving to South Dakota, that there was someone else, Blake stood nervously at the top of the stairs. I knew he wanted to run, but I held him there with pleading eyes that said, *No, I need you here with me. I'm doing this for us.* And that was it. We were finally, officially, a couple.

I landed a job working with immigrant and refugee families new to South Dakota, which gave me and my international experiences purpose, and rented an apartment in Tea, a small city just outside of Sioux Falls, with a friend from college. Blake stayed in Bryant, ninety miles away, commuting to Brookings to complete the class he needed to graduate, working with his dad and brother on their farm and at the movie theater in the meantime, and serving as a member of the South Dakota Army National Guard. He visited me in Tea a couple times each week, then on weekends, I returned to Bryant, which made Saturdays date nights and Sundays family days with dinner at his Grandma Marilyn's. Guard drill brought him to Sioux Falls one weekend each month, which felt like a glimpse of the future: Blake returning from a day of work, me greeting him with his favorite meals—Reuben sandwiches, chicken Alfredo, tater tot hotdish. When he watched me fry burgers and caramelize onions simultaneously in preparation for patty melts, he seemed impressed. "I would have burned everything if I tried to do all that at once."

But he impressed me, too, when he asked if he could make beef stroganoff. We were settling into our relationship against the backdrop of years of friendship and shared history. It felt natural. It felt solid and secure.

And then, one day that winter when I slipped out onto the patio to smoke a cigarette from the not-so-secret stash Blake, my roommate, Amy, and I sneaked from a couple of times a week, the first puff brought on a wave of nausea. I stubbed the cigarette out. That weekend, I met my mom and sister for a shopping day. When I commented that I needed to look at bras—mine all seemed to have shrunk in the wash—my mom laughed and said, "Yeah, maybe they shrunk, or maybe you're pregnant."

I bought a test on my way home. It was positive. Blake and I were having a baby.

I couldn't tell him the results over the phone, I reasoned. Better to wait just a few days until he visited. And no reason to push him to come sooner, no ominous *I-have-something-to-tell-you*. That would only worry him, and I didn't need that. I needed time.

I was nervous. Not nervous about the baby. Nervous about

Blake. We'd talked about moving to Alaska—he'd applied for a job at an Army base there, and I'd applied to graduate school—but we hadn't made official marriage plans, much less planned for kids. I teetered back and forth between confidence and uncertainty, wondering if the roots of our relationship were established firmly enough to support this. Blake didn't have a full-time job; he was just finishing school. We lived an hour and a half apart. But he loved kids. I knew that from Sunday dinners at his Grandma's, where cousins climbed his limbs like a jungle gym. I pictured Blake hunting ants on the deck with my roommate's toddler son. Still, a child of our own was something else, entirely.

When Blake finally came that week, I held out for as long as I could. We ate supper, then settled on the couch, him sitting across from the TV, me reclining against his chest. I tuned out the adult cartoons he was watching, instead tracing the seam of his Levis with my thumb, wondering how to begin. I still hadn't found the starting place when we went to bed but knew I could never tell him in the rush of the morning—me getting ready for work, him leaving early for Bryant—so, I had to get it out before he fell asleep.

I lay on my side, studying Blake's profile in the shadows cast by parking lot lights filtered through blinds. I focused on the comforting way darkness softens edges, the steady rise and fall of his breath. Propping myself up on my left elbow, I laid my right hand across his chest and whispered, "I have to tell you something." When he lifted his chin in my direction, I rested my temple against his bare chest. I closed my eyes, breathed in his soapy scent, and said, "We're having a baby."

Blake squeezed me with the right arm that was wound under me and around my waist. He kissed my hairline. I waited for words. Instead, I felt his left arm reach down to meet his right, a gentle hug. I blinked my eyes open, turned my face toward his, found him smiling. He pressed his full lips against my thin ones. Still no words.

"So, you're OK?" I asked. "That doesn't scare you?"

He squeezed me again. "Oh, it's terrifying," he laughed. "But of course, I'm fine, everyone loves a baby." I marveled at the simplicity. In these strong, unpredicted winds, he hadn't swayed. "What about you," he asked. "How are you?"

"Tired," I said. "And sick." He moaned an apology. I laced my fingers with his. Sliding our hands over my stomach, laying them flat, as if there were something there to feel, I added, "but happy." I whispered, "Can you believe we're having a baby?"

Blake's answer was a drowsy whisper, "I can't believe how lucky I am," and a faint squeeze of my hand. He kissed my forehead, and I settled into contented silence.

A week later, Blake offered a shy proposal in the apartment living room, pulling a paper bag with a jewelry box inside out from under the couch. I didn't know until years later that sometime between the news of the pregnancy and his awkward proposal he had asked his dad and brothers to go for a drive. When he told them the news of the baby, they pulled to the side of the gravel road, and my soon-to-be father-in-law, Mark, and Blake's oldest brother, Brock, celebrated with a finger-snapping, feet-flailing dance *a la* Rodney Dangerfield in *Caddyshack*, then they all drove to Watertown to buy an engagement ring. Even without the backstory, I laughed at Blake's less-than-romantic proposal, but it was a warm laugh that tinged my cheeks pink. His shyness was one of the things I loved about him.

But it also made him hard to read.

When Blake called one night, I attempted the usual small talk, and he resisted. This wasn't unusual, exactly. As comfortably as we'd settled into our relationship, he could still feel distant sometimes. Conversation didn't always come naturally. But this phone call was not stunted by an awkward silence. This was strained silence, broken finally with a rush of words. "I can't drive down there tonight," he said, "and I know I shouldn't tell you this over the phone, but it really can't wait."

My response was slow, lilted. "OK?" I froze by the kitchen table, steadied myself on a chair.

Blake's voice rumbled like radio static. "Amber, my unit's being activated."

"Your what?" I blinked at the words. My cell phone burned my cheek. "What do you mean?"

"My guard unit," he explained. "I'm being deployed." The word rang in my ears as Blake added, "To Iraq."

I nodded involuntarily, like a disrupted bobble head doll. *Deployed* meant *gone*. *To Iraq* meant *to war*. Reality took shape. "When?"

"This summer," Blake whispered.

My stomach hollowed, as if I'd just sped over a hill, the road dropping out from under me. I swayed. "How long?"

"Twelve months."

Tears filled my eyes as months became math equations, our life a story problem. *If a soldier is deployed in July and his child is due in October, how old will the child be when his dad returns from a twelve-month deployment?*

If his dad returns.

My head bobbing shifted, side-to-side, as I studied my own naivety. How could I forget this possibility? How could words like *activation* and *deployment* sneak up on me? The first traces of our love were letters mailed from South Dakota to Fort Sill, Oklahoma, during Basic Training and AIT. Our first kiss came on the Fourth of July, under a cottonwood tree, and our relationship rekindled on

Memorial Day Weekend. I'd rehearsed my role as Blake's something-to-come-home-to on drill weekends. I knew *soldier* was a significant part of his identity. But when I started to imagine him as husband and father, when I shifted my focus to the planning of a wedding and the picking of baby names, I'd forgotten about that part of the script. Until that moment when *soldier* became a defining characteristic, *war* an eminent reality.

I don't remember how the rest of the conversation played out, but I'm sure Blake apologized, reassured. I'm sure I had little to say, not knowing what questions to ask. The news caught me off guard. I felt like I'd been walking along on a sunny winter day, relishing in its warmth, when I hit a patch of ice and felt my feet slip out from under me. The sudden shift screamed dangerous potential—broken wrist, concussive blow of skull on sidewalk—but then I re-oriented myself, reflexively lowering my center of gravity, curling myself into a protective stance. I fought off overwhelming emotion with logic: sometimes deployments dissolved, orders changed. Many assignments were safe. Boring, even. All the soldiers I could think of in my family and our community had returned safely from war.

By the time Blake said, "I'm sorry. I know I shouldn't have told you over the phone. I didn't think I should wait."

I recovered enough to deflect his apology.

"No, it's OK," I said. "You needed to tell me."

I knew his was sincere regret, even though I also knew he was probably relieved that he didn't have to look me in the eye when he gave me the news or watch the words wash over me. If he'd come to tell me in person, he might have invited me to go for a drive, let the highway serve as an excuse to avoid eye contact. But I knew he believed it when he promised, "Everything will be all right."

ON MEMORIAL DAY WEEKEND, exactly one year after I moved

home from Mexico, Blake and I were married. In the ceremony, after we exchanged our vows, my voice quivered as I sang, "More than the greatest love the world has known, this is the love I give to you, alone." I'm sure Blake struggled with the intimacy of eye contact as the song culminated in the lyrics I'd adapted to match my true sentiment. The original version read *I know I've never lived before*, but I changed it. I felt like I had lived. I had explored. I had allowed myself to become different, to live abroad, to find out who and what was important to me, and so when I returned to South Dakota and to Blake, I was sure. His impending deployment didn't change that, maybe even reinforced it. As sappy as it sounds, our relationship felt scripted. Meant to be. So, I sang, "I know I've never loved before, and my heart is very sure no one else could love you more."

After the wedding, we settled into a temporary existence. My aunt Avis and uncle Ron offered to us the seventies ranch they'd purchased to renovate for their future retirement home as our own temporary, retro honeymoon suite. Living rent-free, two blocks from both my parents' house and Blake's dad's, offered a perfect balance of connection and privacy until Blake would leave in July for pre-deployment training. The only imperfection was the sense of temporariness. Instead of newlyweds, settling into our lives together, we were squatters. We filled the cupboards with ramen and canned soup—no spices or dry ingredients for baking—the fridge with sandwich meat and cheese, a few cans of pop and beer. If we were settlers on the open prairies of Eastern South Dakota, this would have been our dug out, cut into the side of a shallow hill. Just enough space to provide shelter and protect us from the elements. A place to begin, but not enough resources or time before winter would set in to begin building a solid future.

Since I was on break from school and Blake had abandoned job hunting at news of the deployment, we divided our days between Blake's family and mine, between time together and time apart. I didn't want Blake to feel suffocated, like marriage had ripped him from his routine of farming and hunting and baseball. I didn't want to force him into an uncomfortable abandoning of everything that had been important to him up until that point, because he would be uprooted from all of it and all of us so soon. We loafed through those weeks, sleeping in, sharing sandwich and ramen lunches before deciding what to do with the rest of our day. On a typical Saturday, while Blake golfed with his dad and brothers or tinkered with farm machinery, I went shopping or rummaging with my mom and sister. The hobby had taken on new meaning since my sister and I were both expecting—my first child, Erin's second. We hunted for twenty-five cent onesies and pristine baby toys like Blake and his brothers hunted for deer sheds, all of us searching out potential in our own way.

When I came home with a wobbly, white bookshelf missing half its paint, I exclaimed, "A dollar. Can you believe it?"

Blake tested its frame with his fingertips. It swayed. "You mean they paid you a dollar to take it, right?"

I set to work on the bookshelf the next day. As I crouched in the driveway, adding a few screws to tighten its frame and just enough paint to make its shabbiness chic, Blake, who'd spent the morning putzing around with his dad and his brothers, pulled into the driveway. He jumped out of the driver's seat, testing the bookshelf with a jab of fingers, and when it didn't give, he smiled. From the passenger seat, Brock laughed, "Those suckers. This thing's gotta be worth at least two dollars, now."

I scoffed. "Two? I could get at least ten."

"Amber isn't a junker like Grandpa Bob," Blake said. "She's not just filling up a shed with junk so that when she's gone, we can have a huge auction. She's a flipper. It's all about investment."

I leaned into him, laughing. "It's all about potential."

Blake, never comfortable with public displays of affection, squeezed me quickly, then stepped away. "Do you still have work to do here? Or are you done with your project for today?"

I squatted, using the handle of my paintbrush to tap the paint lid into place. "I was just gonna clean up, let this paint dry, then get this gem put away so it doesn't get rained on. Why what are you up to?" I squinted up at Blake, his tan face half hidden by a seed corn cap.

"Tree wrangling," he smiled. "I'll drop Brock off, then come pick you up."

I nodded, as if I knew what that meant, like I did when someone gave directions to somewhere—the old Anderson place, or two miles east of Three Buck slough—it seemed like something a South Dakota farm girl should know.

When Blake pulled in the driveway in his dad's truck, I jumped in. We snaked from the smooth finish of the state highway to the cracked pavement of a county road, heading south toward my Grandma Betty's old farm, then veered left on to gravel. Blake drove slowly, scanning the roadside. When he came to a stop and bounded into the ditch, I followed, realizing when dry grass scratched my thighs that for a South Dakota girl, I hadn't come prepared. *There's a reason farmers always wear jeans*, I thought, as my pale skin turned pink and began to itch.

In the shade of a shelterbelt, Blake combed through brome and switchgrass with his hand. I meandered behind him, plucking handfuls of stems, letting them scatter. When he crouched to inspect something, I peered over his shoulder. Blake glanced up. "Can you grab the spade from the back of the truck?" I nodded, then climbed the steep embankment of the ditch. At the truck, I hoisted myself up on the rear bumper to reach the spade. "And a bucket. Grab a bucket or two, if you can."

When I made my way back to Blake, he had pulled grasses in a six-inch circle, and trampled a larger circle beyond that, isolating a spindly tree. "Do you want to dig?" His voice and his eyebrows rose in anticipation as he offered this opportunity to me.

"The tree?"

"Yeah. It's a spruce. They transplant pretty well. Do you want to dig?" I stifled a smile as I shook my head no and offered him the spade. I'd known Blake essentially all of his life, and despite my I-know-who-I-married mantra, usually a reminder to myself when he spent more time golfing or hunting than I might deem necessary, this side of Blake—this finder and saver/stealer of trees—was new to me. I found it endearing.

"So this is what you're after?" I asked, as he placed the sapling and its clump of roots and dirt in the five-gallon bucket at my feet. "Spruce trees?"

"Yeah, they usually take pretty good when you move them," Blake shook his head, "but the deer. I have to keep replanting the row along the highway at Glen's, because the deer nip them off before they get established." I pictured the farm place a mile east of Bryant, where Glen and Pauline's house used to stand. Glen and Pauline were Jensen's, too, though unrelated to Blake's family. Still, they were the kind of small town community members that felt like relatives, and so when Blake's Jensen clan bought the acreage and repurposed the outbuildings to house their farm machinery, a four-wheeler, a mower, and other odds-and-ends, it seemed natural. Along the highway ran a stand of small trees, some dead, one maybe six feet tall but stripped of branches near its base, others smaller, struggling to survive.

"Seems like a lot of work," I teased, tilting my head to study

Blake as he pitched the spade down into the ground, set the blade with his foot, then pulled back to unearth another sapling.

He shrugged. "What else have we got to do?" Blake caught a glimpse of my smile and asked, "What? You think it's weird?"

"Not at all. It's just different than it sounds," I said. "Tree wrangling sounds tough, like steer wrestling or something. But it's really kinda sweet."

Blake ignored my teasing and worked his way forward, wrangling trees. When I asked if digging trees from ditches was legal, he paused and raised his eyebrows and palms in question, lifting and lowering his hands as if testing the balance of right and wrong.

I laughed, "So I should have worn running shoes, in case we get caught?"

He shrugged and nodded slightly, acknowledging the possibility. "Or we can just call it good for today, go plant these, then bring out buckets of water—give them a good soak in case we don't get rain. That should give 'em a good chance."

On the drive to Glen's, I encouraged conversation, asking Blake, "So, what's your favorite kind of tree?" I wanted to deepen this new knowledge of him, soak the roots of our relationship, encouraging growth that would anchor us further.

"If I'm being practical, probably a cottonwood." His answer cued an image of silver-green leaves, the whisper of their rustling leaves. He turned the question to me. "You?"

"Never really thought about it," I admitted. "I know I hate those trees with the brown seed pods—they were everywhere on our farm." I reminisced about family vacations to Custer State Park, winding up Needles highway, stopping to climb round boulders that seemed extra-terrestrial to me as a child, the ground a blanket of pine needles, and my mom snapping photos of trees with interesting knots in their roots or twisted trunks.

Then I said, "I guess I like those trees you see out in the Black Hills, growing out of rocks. I don't know what kind of trees, even, but I like how they grow out of nothing." If I'd paused to consider the metaphorical implications of trees taking root in less-than-ideal conditions, the image might have offered comfort. Instead, as we pulled into the driveway and onto the grass next to the row of trees Blake was trying so hard to establish, I worried over uprooted saplings and survival rates. Tears formed at the image of our own eminent uprooting.

Blake pulled me from the sad spiral of my thoughts when he said, "You know, that wasn't true, about the cottonwood." I turned to face him as he continued. "If I'm dreaming big, my favorite is an oak." I lifted my chin in his direction, interest piqued. "They're more expensive and hard to grow, but once they're established, they're around for hundreds of years."

I smiled at the sound of *hundreds of years*. As I considered the landscape around us, the generational legacies linked to homesteads, the family stories that linked us to the landscapes around us, my thoughts shifted from fear and uncertainty to possibility. We planted our wrangled trees, watered them, and willed their roots to take hold, then headed back to our temporary home to take shelter while we could.

Two

WHEN BLAKE SAID, "WE NEED AN APARTMENT," it might have seemed like a perfectly appropriate newlywed activity. Upsizing, settling in, as we prepared for the birth of our first child. But Blake was leaving for Fort Dix, New Jersey, for pre-deployment training in two days. An apartment seemed unnecessary.

We didn't know how long pre-deployment training would last, but from Blake's perspective, it couldn't be short enough. Their twelve-month deployment clock wouldn't start ticking until they were officially overseas. Fort Dix was wasted time, in his mind. For me, stateside was reassuring. I secretly hoped for three months, so Blake could come home when our son was born. But there was no certainty. We were living on Army time, which left two options: plan but prepare for contingencies or forget planning all together, hurry up and wait. I opted for the latter, putting off Lamaze classes because I couldn't be sure who would be in the delivery room with me. If birthing plans were optional, certainly an apartment could wait too.

"Can't I do that later?" I asked, adding silently, *after you're gone.*

Blake apologized. "I wish we could, but we need to find an apartment. Today."

I laughed, but he wasn't kidding. "We need to sign a lease before I leave," he explained. "If I don't have paperwork, we won't get housing credit. It would be a big deal, financially." Apartment hunting was suddenly our top priority.

We bought a newspaper, and while Blake drove us to Sioux Falls, where I would return to work once the school year began, I circled leads in the classifieds.

First, we toured sketchy income-based housing complexes. One landlord promised that the hole punched in the wall would be patched before we moved in. We feigned smiles as we pulled back loose oven doors and stepped over stained carpet. As we drove between potential apartments, I tried not to cry. Blake pretended not to notice, but when my cousin called, he answered, telling her I wasn't available. I heard her skeptical laugh—"If she's in the bathroom, I can wait."—followed by Blake's firm, if nervous, explanation that I'd call her later. When she persisted—"Blake, are you joking? Are you turning in to some kind of control freak?"—I couldn't help but smile.

When he hung up, I wiped away tears and thanked him. "But you realize she probably thinks you've murdered me or something."

"Oh, absolutely," he agreed. "Probably dialing 911 right now. But I was pretty sure you didn't want to talk."

I laughed, then burst into tears. "Well, every time I try, this happens, so yeah, I don't think it would have gone well."

Our next stop was an apartment complex called Canterbury Estates. If the name didn't tip us off, the hotel-style lobby and hallways lilting with classical music should have warned that we didn't belong there. I couldn't imagine a child crying in those communal spaces. The manager tiptoed around the same concern, glancing at my six-month-pregnant belly and asking, as we rode the elevator up to the second floor, who would be inhabiting the apartment. Blake waved a flat palm in my direction and answered, "Her," then paused before adding, "and the baby."

At that point, we should have thanked her and said our goodbyes. Instead, Blake worked on emphasis and prolonged awkwardness. "Her and the baby," he repeated, adding, "but not me. I won't be here." The manager blinked, glanced at my tearful red eyes, then back at Blake. The tour was brief. No discussion of amenities. She mentioned the price of rent, just to confirm that we couldn't afford a one bedroom, and we moved on to the last apartment on our list: a two-bedroom on Marion Road.

As we pulled into the parking lot, I noticed a swing set and basketball courts between the main building and what appeared to be a bike trail. The building wasn't brand new, but new enough. Blake was optimistic. "Let's hope this place is as good as it looks from the outside."

The landlord was friendly and straightforward. She pointed out underground parking, a pool and workout room as we made our way upstairs. The hallways were clean and quiet with signs of life: welcome mats and wreaths adorning doors. The apartment smelled clean, and its stain-free carpet and in-unit laundry balanced out its pressed wood cupboards and vinyl flooring. But I was exhausted, and when the landlord offered to leave us for a few minutes so we could talk things over, I leaned against the living room wall and slid down. Blake followed. He gave me a few moments of silence before saying, "I hate to push, here, Amber, but what do you think?"

"I don't know," I answered. Tears came quickly. "I just can't handle it. I don't want an apartment for *me*. It is supposed to be for *us*." I slid my hips forward until my lower back lay against the floor. My stomach rose visibly as the baby did a barrel roll and wedged himself under my ribs. I inhaled and placed my hand over the uneven bulge. "I never pictured it like this."

Blake acknowledged my discomfort, asking, "What's the little jerk doing now? Do we need to find you a pop can or something?"

The little jerk was a term of endearment for our unborn son. The pop can was a trick I'd read about: holding a cold can against the stomach to get the little jerk to move when he was positioned awkwardly. "Should I have a talk with him?" Blake asked. "Tell him who's boss? You don't want him getting too uppity even before he's born."

"I'll be fine," I laughed. "But you should be careful who you refer to 'the little jerk' in front of, you know. That's all that was missing from your little speech over there at Canterbury Estates."

"I never would've said that," Blake objected.

I rolled my eyes in his direction, expecting to encounter feigned innocence, instead finding a tense but tired face. He couldn't stand this uncertainty. "Well, maybe you wouldn't have said that," I teased, "but how many times did you tell her that I'd be living there alone, at least, until I had the kid." I lowered my swollen eyelids in mock disapproval. "You know she thought I was your mistress, expecting your illegitimate child."

"Yeah, that wasn't very smooth," Blake admitted.

"And the look on her face..."

He nodded in agreement, "Like '*Who are these two idiots?*'"

"And she didn't even know our son was a jerk."

Blake smiled. I rested my head on his arm. "It wouldn't have mattered," he said. "We all knew we were never gonna live there."

"Yeah," I sighed. "*We* never were." I immediately regretted the emphasis.

Blake stood, paced the living room a couple times before pausing at the sliding doors leading out to a small balcony. "I know this isn't the way you pictured it, Amber, but we need an apartment, and I actually like this place." He stopped beside me and offered me a hand. Pulling me up, he said, "With the underground parking, you'd never have to scrape your windows in winter, and

I wouldn't have to worry about you slipping on ice when you're lugging a car seat around."

I was touched.

And I had to admit, "I like the walk-in closet."

Blake nodded. "So should we go for it? Sign the lease? I promise not to make it sound like you're having an illegitimate child." I agreed with a nod. "I'll keep it simple," he promised. "This is my wife. She's an idiot. But I'm an even bigger idiot. And our unborn son's a jerk."

THE NEXT DAY, after the successful apartment hunt and an emotional going-away party, Blake and I drove back to Sioux Falls. I stared out the window, turning from him to hide the tears in my eyes. I willed my breath to rise and fall steadily, resisted choking sobs. My mind raced, searching for things to say—reassuring things that would convince Blake that I was fine—but if I spoke, I knew I would cry. I reached awkwardly behind me to rest my hand on his thigh. When he wasn't shifting gears, he laid his hand over mine.

I was surprised when Blake parked in a gravel lot. I looked up to see a paved road curving up toward the Armory. The building, buzzing with cars and people, must have been over half a mile away. When we stepped out of the truck, I walked to Blake and leaned into him, inhaling the scent of his uniform, trembling as I exhaled. "Should we head up there?" I asked, nodding toward the building.

Blake pulled me closer. "No," he whispered. Leaning his cheek against the top of my head, he said, "Let's say goodbye here." I felt confused. Clearly there were families, clinging to their last moments together. It seemed irresponsible to relinquish even a moment with Blake. He explained, "That'll only make it harder. All those people. Army chaos." I imagined wives, children crying. "Here it's just us," he said. This distance was Blake's way of protecting me, and I was too tired to object.

Lifting myself up on tiptoes, I leaned into him, resting my temple against his grainy, close-shaven cheek, wondering how I would manage to stand without his body there to support me. "It'll be all right," Blake assured me. "It really will. I promise, it will be all right."

I repositioned myself, pressing my forehead against his, trying to believe him, but tears streamed from my pinched eyes, my nose dripped. I pulled back, embarrassed.

"I'm sorry, I know I shouldn't…"

"Don't be sorry," Blake said. "You have every right to be sad." But I could feel the tension in his muscles, the way his back stiffened with each of my sobs. I knew I was making this more difficult for him, and that was the last thing I wanted. I didn't need him worrying about me.

When another car pulled into the gravel lot, Blake inhaled a long, slow breath. A uniformed soldier stepped out, pulled a duffle bag from the trunk, then slammed it shut. As if the sound had wakened him from a dream, Blake exhaled, hugged me firmly, and said he'd better go.

I panicked. "I'll come with you." I offered, again.

"I know," Blake said, hugging me. "But it's not gonna get any easier." He pulled back to look me in the eye. "It's really better here, just us. I don't want anyone else."

With our hands clasped at our sides, we leaned in, forehead to forehead again for just a moment, eyes closed, and Blake released me. He nodded. I smiled through tears as he lifted his rucksack from the bed of the truck and, without looking back, met the other soldier a few paces ahead in the dirt parking lot.

"Sucks, huh?" the soldier sighed.

Blake nodded.

"Gonna be a real shit show in there."

He nodded again.

And then I watched Blake walk away from me, further and further, until his figure disappeared into a crowd of soldiers and family members and there was nothing left for me to do but get in the truck and drive home.

When I got to the highway, I realized I'd driven in the wrong direction. Or maybe I simply didn't know which direction to go. Home wasn't the apartment Blake and I had hunted for—the lease didn't start until August. Home wasn't my apartment in Tea—I hadn't stayed there since the wedding. But I couldn't return alone to the temporary home I'd shared with Blake, and I didn't want to return to my parents' house. I pulled into a Burger King parking lot to cry.

Slumped against the steering wheel, I let tears stream down my face. I let my shoulders shake, let sobs catch in my throat and bark their way out. With no one watching, I fell apart.

And then, I put myself back together.

I pulled out of the parking lot, and instead of backtracking to the interstate we came in on, I drove back roads I wasn't familiar with, reminding myself that I knew the general direction I was headed, that if I kept going north, I would hit Interstate Highway 229, and from there, I would find my way.

A MONTH LATER, Blake's brothers and dad helped me move into the apartment, and I put myself to work establishing another temporary home—this time for myself and my soon-to-be-born son. I stitched gauzy, green and white fabric into curtains, my foot lifting, Grandma Betty's old sewing machine halting, as I reversed my stitch, then let the needle fly forward once more to the fabric edge. My mom taught me to sew even before it was a subject in seventh grade home economics, and both of my grandmas were quilters, commemorating graduations, marriages, and births with their creations and stitching together less beautiful but functional crazy quilts for Lutheran Women's organizations. These generations of women taught me the importance of back stitching, of securing the seams of what we create. I pulled aside the finished curtains and trimmed threads before heading into the master bedroom to put my work in place.

The bed, delivered from the furniture store earlier that day, was dressed with wedding gifts: olive green, Egyptian cotton sheets, thin down blanket, fine-quilted white comforter. I slid the curtains over an iron rod, then lifted them into place, and noticed my mistake: the curtain hem angled slightly but steadily, so that the right side hung almost two inches lower than the left. I shrugged it off. No one would see them, tucked away in the master bedroom of the apartment I lived in, alone. I stepped into the hallway and switched off the bedroom light.

As I moved through the hall, Blake smiled at me from an antique frame perched on an old ladder with chipping white paint. In the living room, I settled in on my new sectional couch, its cushions still firm, and fabric still smelling faintly of the protective plastic it was delivered in. Blake peered out from a wedding portrait framed in old barn wood. I scanned the room. New TV, primitive bench for a stand. New couch. Antique artist's desk. I was piecing together past and present to construct a future.

Blake was one of the new pieces. His possessions still lived at his dad's house: T-shirts, dingy socks, and carpenter jeans with worn knees lining the drawers of a dresser in his old bedroom up-stairs; trophy deer and Carhartts hanging in the garage; a baseball uniform, unwashed after the last game he played in July, stuffed in a duffle bag downstairs. His life up to that point had not been lived with me; his present was being lived out in military barracks. In that apartment, he was an accessory. A decoration perched on the wall. Still, we'd known each other all our lives, and our families shared history—grandmothers serving Ladies Aid dinners together long before either of us were born, fathers and uncles playing on the same baseball teams. We were a combination of old and new, and our future held promise.

As the baby's due date approached, I filled a changing table with newborn diapers, wedged baby wipes and diaper cream in between. I folded burp rags and onesies and sleepers, a sweater vest that I'd teased Blake our son had to wear. "If we're gonna name him George, he needs V-necks and bowties."

My hope filled a closet with clothes Blake might wear someday: thin-wale corduroys and plaid button-ups for some future job, soft long-sleeve T-shirts and flannel pajama pants for lounging on the couch.

When Blake called the last week of September, saying the Army had granted him a "family weekend" before heading overseas, I was ecstatic. We would have two days together. A short reprieve from separation. A small store of connection to draw upon during deployment. I bought a new pair of maternity jeans and a red, eyelet lace top with capped sleeves that made me feel pretty, even at thirty-eight weeks pregnant. It was a frivolous investment, especially since I secretly hoped I'd go into labor two weeks early so that Blake could be at the birth. But that didn't happen. We spent our time in Bryant, sleeping at my parents' house, driving around with Brock, Brad, and Mark, scouting deer for the upcoming archery season, eating Sunday dinner at Grandma Marilyn's. The weekend passed uneventfully but quickly, and on Sunday afternoon, we returned to Sioux Falls for Blake's departure.

I insisted on a stop at the apartment, saying I needed to grab some things, but really I wanted Blake to see the placed furnished and sit on the new couch, be impressed by my knack for interior design, glimpse a home that he could imagine returning to. And I wanted a memory of Blake in the apartment—something more than a picture of him on the wall—to hold in my mind over the coming year.

My decorating didn't prove as fascinating as I'd hoped, and Blake didn't notice my flawed, home-sewn curtains, but he did comment on the couch. "Pretty comfortable," he said, settling in with the remote. As we sat, silent, in front of the TV, Blake put his arm around me. I leaned into him. I wanted to feel content, but my mind raced. This wasn't the joyful memory I'd been hoping to create. This awkward pause, quiet killing of time, felt passive. In the face of separation and stress, my body buzzed with nervous energy. I felt a need for action, a need to busy myself with something. I remembered the crib.

I'd fought with the crib for hours the week before but gave up on balancing awkwardly sized pieces, trying to hold them steady, realizing that with more hands—just a few moments of help from someone else—the pieces would slide easily into place. I stood, intending to ask Blake for help, but he didn't seem to notice when I peeled away from his chest, when his hand slipped from my body to the couch. He stared ahead. The tension in my body escalated to a ringing in my ears. I'd always hated asking for help, always preferred stubborn independence, for better or for worse. So, when Blake failed to acknowledge my movement, my jaw tightened. Without explanation, I retreated to the bedroom.

I rattled instruction sheets dramatically before laying them flat. I noisily propped a crib end against the wall, lifted a side rail to slide it into place. The crib end fell. I laid it flat, lifted the rail at a ninety-degree angle, but I was unsteady. Brackets pulled. Weak, pressed wood threatened to crack. "Damn it," I muttered.

"What are you doing?" Blake called from the couch.

"This crib," I said. "Fucking impossible to put together." I listened for footsteps.

Instead, I heard Blake ask, "Do you have to do it now?"

Not "Can I help you?" Not "What do you need?" I read his lack of concern as a reminder: this crib and this baby and this apartment were my responsibility. I stood, hands on hips, facing the wall. I imagined Blake on the other side, reclined in front of the TV. My shoulders tensed as I imagined letting loose the words that wanted to claw their way out. *If not now, when? Tomorrow, when you're at Fort Dix? Next week, when you're overseas? In two weeks, after our child is born and I'm here with him, alone?* I wanted to say, *Yes, I need to do this now, and I need your help.* But as I glared in Blake's direction, imagined the confrontation, I realized the absurdity. Snapping a crib rail into place would provide no real security. Metaphorically, it might offer protection. Symbolically it might create some sense of preparedness. But nothing Blake or I could say or do would change our future.

He was leaving. In an hour.

Of course he wanted to spend that hour comfortable. Calm. Quiet.

Wordlessly, I returned to the couch, where I curled my knees up, let them spill onto Blake's lap, and lay my head against his chest. I settled into silence, matching my inhales and exhales with the steady beat of his heart.

WHEN WE WALKED HAND IN HAND into the airport, Blake wore civilian clothes: a burgundy polo tucked into olive green cargos, the same ones he'd shown up in three days before, when I smiled and said, "You didn't have to wear your uniform." I wore my new maternity jeans and a white jacket with scalloped edges, cinched over my bulging stomach. With no camouflage to attract strangers' stares, Blake might have been a businessman—a sales rep off to visit a client in a neighboring state, or a manager off to a training—and we might have been a family floating on certainty, with a crib assembled in a nursery painted sea green, a route to the hospital planned, months of happiness ahead. I masked my fear and sadness in that fantasy of what we looked like from the outside.

Very few people travelled through the Sioux Falls Regional airport on a Sunday afternoon in September, but an encounter with each and every one of those travelers was almost ensured in the single-terminal airport with its handful of flight gates and a single corridor of ticket counters. After check-in, we lingered near the airport's lone souvenir shop, kitty-corner from the airport's only café, when I recognized the thin, runner's frame of our high school science teacher, Jim Dorman. I considered ducking into the store, hoping to maintain anonymity, but our eyes met. Jim smiled warmly, already reaching for a handshake as he strode toward us. "Where you guys headed? A little trip somewhere?"

I attempted an answer, but my throat seized, tears collected.

"Actually, just me," Blake said, stepping forward, shielding me from the conversation. "I'm headed back to Fort Dix, then overseas to Iraq." As my tears began to fall, I dipped my cheek to my shoulder to catch them, chiding myself. *You're not doing this again.*

While Blake talked, I unwound my fingers from his and let my hands fall to my sides. I observed the straight trunk of his body and imitated his posture. I fixed my eyes on a rack of dream catchers dangling in the souvenir shop, letting my vision cross slightly, blurring the strings into a tighter weave, and I breathed. I staved off overwhelming ideas like twelve months of deployment, one fatherless year of our son's life, by focusing on increments: two weeks until the due date, the promise of Blake's two-week Rest & Recreation sometime during the deployment, a countdown to Blake's homecoming, and a counting forward, too, to George's first birthday. Instead of worrying about the threat of storms, the possibility of drought, I trusted the promise of growth. By the time Mr. Dorman shook Blake's hand and said, "Well, best of luck to you. Thank you for your service," I was able to look him in the eye and smile. And when it came time for Blake to leave, when he made his promise—"Everything will be all right"—I willed myself to believe him. I hugged him firmly. Like something solid and secure, something sure, I anchored him to home.

TWO WEEKS LATER, as Blake and the rest of Charlie Battery prepared themselves to move from Kuwait into Iraq, I set off on a mission of my own. Mine was a small convoy, a soft convoy, no armored vehicles. My mission: baby.

In the military, my position in the passenger seat would have indicated that I held highest rank, that I was in control, but I didn't feel in control of anything. My dad, in the seat next to me, would have been next in line—my driver—which, I guess, would have made my four-year-old niece, Cami, perched in her car seat behind me, my gunner. She was surprisingly good at her job. As concerns surfaced—*was I prepared to cross this threshold from daughter to mother, wife to parent?*—and morph to sadness—*how could I do this without Blake?*—Cami mowed them down. She chirped from the backseat, "I know how babies are made."

I turned to meet her gaze. "Really, how?"

"God makes them. Kinda like cookies," she answered with gleaming blue eyes, raised eyebrows, emphatic nod. "With flour and sugar and stuff, stirred up in your tummy."

I smiled. "That's a good way to describe it. Do you think

God put any special ingredients in my baby George? Cinnamon, maybe?" I raised my eyebrows. My dad chuckled in the driver's seat. "Maybe some dirt or rocks, 'cause he's a boy?"

Cami wrinkled her nose. "Or raisins."

"Ewww, raisins?" I shook my head. "Maybe chocolate chips."

"Yeah," Cami giggled. She leaned forward, straining against the straps of her car seat and squinting at me. "But how will George get *out* of your tummy?"

"Hmm," I stalled. "I guess the doctor will help him out." A simple but honest answer.

"Yeah," she continued cautiously, "but usually it's different." She was leaning forward, her white hair swinging around her face as she strained to see mine. "Usually babies are born from somewhere," she hesitated, "somewhere down here." She was lifting her left leg slightly and circling her fingers, held flat and tight together like a model on a commercial for hand cream, near the lower buckles of her car seat. "Somewhere like your bottom." I raised my eyebrows, disguising amusement as surprise. "I know because my mom and I watch baby stories on TV."

"That's very true," I said. "There are two ways for babies to be born."

I muffled a smile into my pillow propped up against the passenger door. But as that silent laugh bubbled up, so did a nervous tremor. I didn't feel much more educated on the process of childbirth than Cami. I'd watched baby stories on TV, too, and had flipped through books about childbirth, but I'd avoided Lamaze classes because I didn't want to sit alone on a mat while other expectant mothers leaned back into their husbands' arms, and those husbands caressed their wives' full bellies. Dr. Wierda had offered taped classes that I could watch in a private hospital room, but I'd fast-forwarded through them, flipping through a magazine as breathing techniques blurred across the screen. It was a relief when she suggested a C-section, because that meant no water breaking, no wondering if I could drive myself to the hospital or if my sister (my birthing partner) would make it in time for the delivery. But with the scheduled procedure just hours away, relief vanished. The doctor would take charge of the delivery, but I would take over the role of parent, alone. Once the surface cracked, fears rushed in. Blake would miss the delivery, but what else? Connection? Miraculous appreciation? Could those things be regained? I wrapped my arms tighter around the pillow, my whole body contracting, pulling in on itself as if cinched by a drawstring, as if I could consume the pillow entirely, as if that would fill me somehow.

Cami broke the silence, again, her voice loosening the pull. "Amber, I'm so excited to meet baby George."

When I turned to smile back at her, I remembered that I was still living in Mexico when Cami was born. I'd missed her birth and over two years of her life, studying them remotely, through emailed photos. Now, almost two years later, she adored me. We frosted cookies together at Christmas, decorated eggs at Easter. She stole the phone from her mom each time I called. On car rides with me, she requested Ray Charles, and we sang "Hit the Road Jack" at the top of our longs and belted out "I've Got a Woman." I'd been thousands of miles away when she was born, but we were connected. Absence was forgotten. Maybe I didn't need to worry.

"I'm excited, too," I agreed. "And I bet baby George can't wait to meet you."

A FEW HOURS LATER, I was dressed in a hospital gown, my wrist bound in a plastic band, and a matching one a fourth its size waiting to cinch the ankle of my soon-to-be-born son. The other adult-sized band hung around the freckled skin of my sister's thin wrist. My dad paced the hallway, shuffling between the doorway and the waiting room with cups of coffee for my mom and sister. My three-month-old nephew slept in his car seat next to a mauve vinyl couch, while his sister danced, sloshing around the sea creatures inside the crib toy she couldn't wait to give George, incessantly pressing the button that initiated its lullaby. With no reason to pace the room like expectant mothers I'd seen on TV, no labor to move along, I lay still, observed the circus around me, and listened to the anxious hum in my ears.

When my cell phone fluttered on the bedside table, I recognized the unknown number as Blake's international call and shook my head in disbelief. I skipped small talk, diving into our conversation with a teasing blow. "Did you mix up the times or something?" I asked, "Because George isn't born yet."

"No, I meant to call you now," Blake said, vowels as broad as the smile I imagined lifting his cheeks and narrowing his eyes. "I may have traveled halfway around the world just to avoid being in the delivery room," he said, laughing at his own favorite joke, "but I still wanted to talk to you before he was born."

"No, seriously," I insisted, "you mixed up the time."

"Nope," he said. "Swear to God." Then he relented, "My section chief might have helped me remember, might have lent me his phone, but I did mean to call you now." As I laughed, someone snapped a photo, and I shooed away the intrusion, wanting to share the moment only with Blake. I didn't realize how thankful I would later be for that image: me on the phone, face flushed and grinning, Blake's presence suggested within the frame of the day. I don't remember the conversation, but I remember the burning muscles in my cheeks, atrophied by months of worry, now tired from smiling deeply. Excitement spread through my body, like the epidural I would soon receive, numbing fears. "Our son will be here so soon. *Our son.*"

"I know," Blake said. "Pretty hard to believe."

When a nurse interrupted to prep me for surgery, my breath shallowed, lips quivered, throat turned to sand paper, calm suddenly depleted. "Well, I guess it's time," I said, pleating the hem of my hospital gown between my fingers. "They've gotta get me ready for surgery."

"Then I'll talk to you in a few hours," Blake said. His exhale was an audible burst, as if he'd breathed into a microphone held too close. I pictured his full lips close to the phone, his eyes pinched slightly, framed by wrinkles. "So," he paused before adding, "good luck."

"Thanks," I said. I stared at the white sheet folded neatly at my knees, ran my hand over the crease. "I love you."

"I love *you*," Blake said with a heavy *you*, like he always did.

I lowered the phone to my lap but couldn't bring myself to push the button that would end the call. I studied the clouded face of the phone, the fleshy haze of makeup its surface had collected from my cheek. I massaged the warm plastic and faux leather of the case as if I could work free some lingering whisper of Blake's voice. I fixed my gaze there, avoiding the eyes of my mom, my sister, and the nurse who checked me over and scribbled in my chart. I cradled the phone, still as warm as Blake's breath would have been if he were there beside me whispering, "Everything will be fine."

But I had to leave behind that warmth when a nurse wheeled me down a corridor, into an elevator, into a stainless-steel room. I tried to imagine Blake beside me in a blue surgical gown, eyes darting side to side between the elastic of his puffy blue cap and the white of his surgical mask. The stubborn image that came instead was Blake, tall and resolute in his Army uniform, clutching the beret he hated wearing in a hand that dangled at his side. I resisted, conjuring Blake's slender frame in baseball pinstripes, his thin hair matted with sweat from his cap, but that image skittered away when a voice instructed me to move to a cold, hard table, scoot to the edge, lean forward, and relax. I followed orders.

After the epidural, and after a blue curtain was draped over my waist, my sister entered the operating room. I thought that with two children of her own, one born via C-section, she was probably more prepared for the role of birthing partner than Blake would have been, and as a medical lab technician, I expected her to be interested in the procedure. She surprised me by ducking into the room and crouching near my head behind the curtain. "I thought you'd be watching the whole thing."

"No way," she said, "not when it's my baby sister they're cutting open." Erin fidgeted with her scrubs, as I imagined Blake would have if he'd been there, but then offered expertise he never would have had. "Remember the heel trick," she said with a wink.

As if on cue, someone dressed in surgical scrubs peered over the curtain at me and said, "Let's see where we're at here. A little pinch to your heel—just let me know if you feel it."

I felt the pinch and nodded. "Yeah, I felt that."

The cheeks behind the surgical mask lifted. "OK, we'll try again in a minute."

My sister had warned me that anesthesiologists know that numbness is setting in, that the patient can't feel the second pinch, so they don't follow through. They go through the motions, ask the question, then laugh as the patient claims to feel a nonexistent pinch. But, a minute later when the nurse anesthetist prepared me for the second pinch, knowledge vanished. I felt it. "Yep," I said. "I felt that."

The masked face peered over the curtain, still smiling. "OK, then, we're ready to go here."

I lifted my head as far off the table as I could, straining my neck to make eye contact with the blue-masked face. I was sure I'd felt it. I could still feel the tingling. I scanned the room for a face that would acknowledge my answer, but the nurses and doctors were all prepping for surgery. My wide eyes met my sister's. She smiled reassuringly. I sucked in icy air, pinched my eyes shut and thought, *Yeah, you can get started. You can cut me open, but I'm gonna scream.* I clenched my teeth and prepared.

And then nothing happened.

I lay on the table, my arms stretched out, crucifixion style, secured with Velcro straps, feeling nothing. No slicing pain, no swelling scream.

I had barely pieced together the sensation of tugging at my abdomen when a nurse announced it was time to get the camera ready. Erin assumed her responsibility, videoing George's first cry and Dr. Wierda's exclamation, "Not much hair here—he's a baldy!" She snapped pictures of George's pursed lips and open-mouthed screams; his clenched fists against the cold metal of a scale that read eight pounds, eight ounces; the slits of his eyes pinched tight beneath a pink and blue striped cap. She recorded everything so Blake could experience the birth of his son in one dimension.

I WAS BACK IN MY HOSPITAL ROOM when my cell phone rang the second time. My family scattered. Someone whispered, "It's Blake," and even the nurse who had come in to check my vitals said she'd come back later. I answered with an exhausted smile, a gentle hello. Blake sounded anxious. "How are you? How's George? How did everything go?"

"We're fine," I said. "Everything went fine. The anesthesia made me nauseous, but it always does."

"I'm sorry," Blake apologized.

"No, don't be," I reassured, remembering the uneasy, almost guilty look on his face whenever morning sickness sent me lurching to the bathroom early in the pregnancy. "It's not a big deal. He's here with me now, wide awake, just looking around."

"Is that normal?"

"I have no idea," I said, laughing. "But it's amazing."

I searched for words to convey the miracle that had just occurred but settled for what I could explain. "He looks just like you," I said, studying the narrow slits of George's eyes. "And your dad says he's got hands like catcher's mitts."

"He's got his Grandpa Win's hands?" Blake exclaimed.

I smiled at his excitement. "That's exactly what your dad said." But it made me sad, too, that Blake had no idea that the body bundled in flannel—the package no bigger and seemingly no heavier than a bread loaf—was so much more impressive than the size of his hands.

Knowing I could never explain, I shifted the conversation to quantifiable things, asking Blake how long he would be in Kuwait. He answered, "I can't say, exactly, but let's just say you and I will probably be traveling at the same time."

"So, you mean, a couple of days?"

"I'm not really supposed to say, but, yeah, you probably won't hear from me for a while, until we get to our next spot."

I stroked the red, flaky skin of George's tightly curled fingers. At some point I said, "He's perfect, Blake."

Blake answered, "I'm sure he is." Then he said in an almost whisper, "Well, I better get going, but thank you. Really, thank you, Amber."

It seemed like a strange thing to say, but I answered, "You're welcome." I set my phone down and clung to George—the closest connection I had to Blake.

Three

I WAS GLAD BLAKE PREPARED ME for the lull in communication because I didn't hear from him for over a week after George was born. Our first conversation was brief.

"I can't talk long, everyone's waiting to call home. I just wanted to let you know we're here now, in Baghdad." He gave me his address. "You can send letters, packages, whatever." He sounded rushed. The phone lagged. But at least I heard his voice.

I sent a package the next day, including a DVD of the delivery. When I talked to him again, he still hadn't received it. And then, another week later when he had, I asked with excitement, "Did you watch the video? What did you think?" Blake responded, "You know, I don't have a computer yet. We tried to watch it in a DVD player, but it didn't work. I'll have to figure something out. But I got the pictures. He has such a perfectly round head."

Our lives were veering in opposite directions. I knew our son in terms of the hot weight of his sleeping body; Blake knew him in terms of hands like catcher's mitts and a perfectly round head. I settled into a routine of diaper changes and feedings and grew accustomed to interrupted sleep; Blake settled into a routine of night missions, daytime sleep, and weekly phone calls to me. Sometimes our conversations were easy, sprinkled with laughter, other times awkward, fumbling, peppered with pauses. Sometimes when I described the marvel of George's eyes widening as he explored shadows and light, the way he worked his mouth into silent Os, Blake seemed to understand or at least to want to. Other times, he seemed unprepared for my stories about the child he hadn't met, the joy he couldn't fully imagine. Sometimes he found things to say about life in Iraq—comments on food or climate, care packages he'd received—but more often he waited for me to talk.

Less than two months into Blake's deployment. I was shopping, when my phone trilled inside my purse. I dug it out and smiled as it flashed "0—unknown." I flipped my hair back, lifted the phone to my ear, and leaned into my shopping cart. Picturing Blake in digital camo, leaning into a payphone, anticipating the deep scratch of his voice, I answered with an intimate, lilted, "Hi."

He must have responded because I moved on to the usual, "How are you?" But then he hesitated, exhaling into the phone. I drew the heavy pause into my lungs and panicked as my voice echoed back to me.

Finally, Blake spoke, his words weighted. "I'm OK," he said. "But something's happened, some guys were hurt."

Unable to absorb the impact of his words, to make sense of the questions swarming my mind, I focused on insignificant details. Steel beams glaring with fluorescent lights. Blue honeycomb cart. I searched for something to say, something appropriate to feel. "I'm so sorry, Blake. Are you...?" I couldn't finish the question. Of course, he wasn't.

He answered anyway. "I wasn't there, on that mission, I'm OK. But it was bad."

I stood between a bright waterfall of women's clothes and shelves lined with towels of blue, green, burgundy, and gold, folded neatly, stacked in fours. I didn't speak. Blake broke the silence. "I just wanted to call before you heard it somewhere else. I wanted you to know I was OK."

"Of course," I fumbled for words. "Blake, I'm so sorry, I don't know what to say."

"I know. There really isn't anything to say."

George must have been snuggled in his car seat right there in front of me as I searched for something to say to the father he hadn't yet met, but I can't picture him there. I must have said something, but I can't remember what. I only remember my hollow throat, a feeling of emptiness, filled suddenly with the thought of my Grandpa Dayton, and how Grandma always said he worried about becoming a father after having experienced war. Would Blake feel the same way? How couldn't he? I lingered on this question, avoiding the scream of a larger fear: what if Blake never *got to be* a father? My eyes followed dingy floor tiles, hoping they would lead me somewhere—backwards in time, maybe, to a wedding dance, where I could lean into Blake's warmth, listen to his off-key rendition of "Desperado," or maybe forward to an airport embrace, to a moment when I could feel Blake's arms locked behind my back, his breath on my neck. Instead, my eyes crossed, blurring the grid of tile into a fuzzy, floating checkerboard. Eventually, Blake said, "Well, I really need to get off the phone. Other guys need to call home."

I'm sure we said goodbye, but all I remember is numbness. I breathed and then blinked as I lifted my eyes. My features felt bloated and heavy, like they do after a deep sleep sometimes. My nose blurred my line of vision, lips felt fat and numb. My chin seemed to spill down over my neck, fingers anchored me to the floor. I moved mechanically—lifting, reaching, lowering—abandoning a package of onesies I'd planned to buy. Then I started to walk, letting the worn wheels of the cart pull me through aisles.

When I made it home somehow, I lifted George from his car seat and paced the living room with him snuggled in my arms. *What if that's our last call? "I'm sorry" was all I could say?* The question echoed like a voice from the hall, a memory of someone else's life.

It was my Grandma Evie's voice. Her story of Grandpa Dayton's tragic death.

Dayton had been working at home, announced a quick trip to town. Just a few errands, home soon. She waved a quick goodbye. But when Dayton neared the train tracks a half-mile south of their farm, where cows had gotten out the day before, Grandma was sure he squinted into the sun to check the fence line. When the train emerged from the grove of trees along the track, he was thirty feet away. He hit the brakes. Too late. Later, Grandma wondered, "Why didn't I go to him? Why didn't I kiss him goodbye?"

I'd always heard those questions as a wish—for one last connection, one last I love you. But after Blake's call, after feeling the threat of tragedy pulse through my body, I understood that she wanted more than a goodbye. If Grandma had stopped Dayton with a kiss, slowed him just a bit, the train would have passed. Tragedy might have been avoided. She wanted to be the something that kept him alive.

As I sat in my apartment, staring at a photo of Blake, playing my own track of regret—*What if this is the conversation I spend the rest of my life reliving?* —and willing myself to be the something that kept Blake alive, I knew it wasn't in my power. And even though my willing, my wishing, was something like a prayer, I couldn't pray for God to save Blake. I had never believed in praying for specific outcomes. Not because I'd witnessed enough good people suffering terrible things to accept that life simply wasn't fair, that challenge and illness and death weren't punishments, simplicity and health and life weren't rewards—I hadn't lived enough to learn that, yet—but because it felt selfish. Two soldiers from Blake's unit were already dead, two more hospitalized and fighting for their lives. I couldn't demand or even hope that my desires be prioritized. Prayer wasn't an act of control but an act of submission. I gave myself over to it.

I tried to imagine those men I didn't know. I pictured Blake and other members of the 147th Field Artillery, American and Iraqi soldiers, their families and their friends, and I prayed for something I couldn't name. Not peace, because that seemed unattainable. Not strength, because they needed more than that, and less than that. I prayed for something like the ability to just get by. To find a way through. To keep moving forward, progressing toward a future where things would get better, someday. Grandma Evie wrote about the days following Dayton's death: how she chose a walnut casket over ornate metal because she knew Dayton loved trees; how when she returned to see him at rest in that casket, he looked peaceful; how she said goodbye, then, knowing that somehow his death had been inevitable—that he'd had to leave— but that she would survive. So that is what I prayed for, wordlessly, my prayer morphing into meditation: a visualization of these families carrying out their lives, carrying on; a channeling of the hum of fear into a positive force, an energy coming from somewhere inside that might feel like numbness but might create an energy, too, to move them forward.

Refocusing my vision, I studied the image of Blake and I from our wedding day, hanging on the wall just above my desk. In the photo, my head tilts slightly, resting against his lapel. We both squint, with serene smiles, into sunlight. Behind us, pillowy white clouds dot a cornflower-blue sky. Feeling connected, somehow, I talked to Blake, tentatively, at first, about how much I missed him, and how scared I was that I wouldn't see him again. I apologized.

And then fear and regret gave way to the warmth of story, a litany of memories—summer nights in the dugout sipping Old Mil Light, a shy marriage proposal, a friend bellied up to the shrimp cocktail bar at our wedding reception—until I arrived back at that moment, the uncertainty we faced. In the near darkness and complete silence of my living room, I reassured my husband. "Blake, if you don't make it home, it will still be enough. Knowing that we were in love, that we were meant to be together, even if for just a little while, that George was meant to be." I grazed my fingertips over my collarbone. "Don't feel bad if you don't make it. Some people never feel as loved in their whole lives as I have felt loved by you."

I LIVED THE WEEKS AFTER THAT PHONE CALL in a fog of fear and gratitude and settled back into a routine of stretches of days in Bryant with family, interrupted by a day or two in Sioux Falls at my apartment when George had well baby visits or I had a follow-ups with my OBGYN. Blake's calls settled back into a weekly routine. I waited for news of Blake's R&R, the two weeks he would have to come home and meet George at some point during the deployment, but Blake warned that he would put it off as long as he could. I couldn't understand how he could prolong the wait to meet his son, but Blake explained that everyone said the best thing about R&R was looking forward to it. That after a trip home, returning to a war zone, things only got harder. I understood the logic. Still, I wanted nothing more than for Blake to hold our infant son. George was my life. My constant responsibility. The deepest love I'd ever experienced. And I wanted to share that with my husband. But for Blake, family and fatherhood weren't at the forefront of his mind. He explained there were two times each day when he allowed himself to think of us—after missions, when his work was done, which was late morning in Baghdad, middle-of-the-night for me, and early evening, during the down time before he prepared for side-by-side night missions with Iraqi police. Evening in Baghdad was morning for me, so Blake's calls usually caught me while I was folding laundry or washing dishes with George napping in his crib, or while I was grocery shopping with George lulled to sleep by the cart's whirring wheels.

One night, when George was asleep on the bed, waiting for me to curl up beside him, and I was sitting at the old artist's desk my mom had given us a wedding gift, scribbling a letter to Blake, he called. I hadn't been able to sleep but didn't realize it was past midnight. I was studying the photo from our wedding day, whispering stories to the image of Blake while I wrote—a habit I'd developed in hopes of making my written voice sound familiar and casual, as if we were talking face-to-face. It seemed almost natural that he had called, as if I'd summoned him, so I didn't think about the fact that Blake had never called so late.

I answered with relief, exhaling "Hey there," as I raised the phone to my ear. I propped my elbows on the desk in front of me. "Perfect timing," I teased. "I'm just finishing a letter to you, so now I'll tell you everything I just wrote, have to throw it away and start again." I squinted at the framed image of Blake, hoping that on the other end of the phone his eyes were narrowing in that same gentle smile.

"Send it anyway," he said. "I always read them more than once. The stories don't get old." He seemed talkative, his voice a punctuated snare drum roll. I leaned into the phone. But then the comfortable silence held on too long, morphing from pause to hesitation, and he laughed, a sort of shrill laugh, but deep and edgy. It scared me. Fear heightened when he said, "So here's a funny war story…"

My ears perked at the phrasing. I froze like a cat sensing the rumbling of a distant storm. I agreed to listen but held my response too long, allowing doubt to creep in, lifting it into a question. "OK?"

"So, the other night," Blake began, "I'm holding the light for the medic, and he's shooting morphine into this Iraqi policeman, this IP, whose got a hole in his guts." I winced at the details, tried to make room among the realities of my daily life—burp rags and blue satin blankets, infant smiles and baby bottles—for the realities of his—Iraqi policemen, medics, morphine. But before I could make sense of the scene he described, before I could ask what, or where, or why, he was reeling forward. "So, we're waiting for the ambulance to show up, and then all the sudden the IP just gets up and says he's gonna walk home."

Blake chuckled and went on. "And so he did. He just got up and walked home."

When Blake chuckled again, I shuddered. I'd never heard him laugh like that before. It was soft, but deep and rumbling, not like the hearty laugh that bubbled from him when he watched cartoons on Adult Swim, or the quick staccato that spilled from him when he'd been drinking. This laugh—this chuckle—thundered inside him, and I felt it rising up through me, seismic waves moving through the mass of my heels and into my body as if the rough edges of a deep fault line were grinding past each other.

I hadn't registered the details of his story. I'd heard the words but hadn't followed the narrative, hadn't recognized any humor— maybe because I wasn't willing to imagine a scene in which my husband stood beside a man with a hole in his guts, much less a reality in which he interpreted that as funny. I stared into the shadowed living room, trembling, trying to release the breath that swelled in my chest, but Blake's laugh held me at the crest. I stopped pacing, sucking in shallow, panicked breaths like I did as a child when the sky grew dark, and I became overwhelmed with worry about thunderstorms and tornados.

Blake must have sensed my confusion, because his laugh was suddenly swallowed up, like the vibrations of a bass drum dampened by a hand. "Why'd I tell you that?" he fumbled. "I can't believe I told you that. I'm so sorry . . . "

My mouth hung open, empty. He apologized again.

But I was sorry, too. For not understanding—again—but also for not trusting him enough at that moment to just ask how he could laugh about a man with a hole in his guts. I was afraid that the answer was a rock forming inside of him, a mass in his chest, the necessary detachment of a soldier, emotions held inside, compressed into callousness. "It's OK," I said. "I'm glad you . . . " But I couldn't finish the sentence.

I didn't know if I was glad he'd told me. I feared the fault line within him, imagined the plates of his experience in Iraq held precariously, felt the threat of those plates slipping, and built-up emotion suddenly releasing.

AS A NEW MOTHER, life pulled me forward through uncertainty with routine: feedings, naps, diaper changes, bath time, sleep. George and I spent days with my sister and her kids; Cami entertained the infants with songs and silly faces. We shopped and took long walks when weather permitted. My parents offered steady support, including babysitting services, regular warm meals of beef and barley soup or sauerkraut stew, and evening entertainment in the form of board games. One night, I sat with my mom at their kitchen table, steam rising from coffee cups as we passed dice back and forth in a heavy leather cup. The house was still, George sleeping on the chambray sheets of his crib, my dad snoring in the living room.

"I'm on a roll here," Mom said. "Going for a Yahtzee."

I inked in open squares on my scorecard and shook my head.

"I can't roll anything. This score might be an all-time low."

"Well, give me a break," mom said, keeping the conversation light. "You usually beat me by a hundred. Tonight just happens to be my night."

I had a reputation of being the gamer in the family: lucky in Yahtzee, a whiz at Rummikub, and so fast at Nertz that skeptics accused me of cheating. But I wasn't feeling lucky that night. I felt sorry for myself, as fear bubbled up. I hadn't talked to Blake in two weeks.

While mom finished her turn, I leafed through old scorecards, some yellowed with age, others stained with water or coffee marks. Most were already claimed, names and nicknames printed in the stylized autographs my sister and I practiced in middle school. If I looked, I knew I could find Blake's sharp cursive. He'd played with mom and I a couple of times. He was terrible at Yahtzee, always rolling for high-scoring combinations, having to zero out half his scorecard. But I wasn't searching for Blake's card that night. I was trying not to think about him. Trying not to be angry. But I was.

Body stiff, shoulders pressed into the spindle-back chair, face pinched, I thought to myself, *There's no way he hasn't had a chance—a minute even—to call me in two weeks.* Each turn, I knocked the dice around in the cup, their sounds imitating the clatter of my thoughts, the stutter of steady gunshots. I spilled dice onto the table, counting black pips like days between phone calls, laboring over each one. Playing the odds of dice falling into required patterns to earn meaningless points, I thought of Blake and the odds he was playing against. I tried to stay fear with statistics and logic: most soldiers make it home alive, and, really, anyone can die any day for any number of reasons. I reminded myself, if Blake was home, I wouldn't sit around worrying about him dying, even though he might suffer a fatal car accident. It really didn't make sense to sit and worry. But I extended the logic: if Blake was at home, commuting to work, I wouldn't have gone two weeks without hearing from him.

Two weeks of silence posed an open-ended question. What if something had happened and I just hadn't heard? I didn't know much about the logistics. When a soldier died, how did the news reach the family? Of course, I'd seen the movie versions of this, but I didn't trust that. Did uniformed soldiers really show up on doorsteps? How long did it take? Did they tell spouses before parents? Or parents before spouses? Spouses, I assumed, but what if it depended on paperwork? If there was a form to fill out, I was sure Blake hadn't updated it. So, if something had happened, maybe the news would reach my father-in-law first. Or my brother-in-law, Brock. Then they would be the ones to tell me. This thought offered a perverse sense of relief. That was all I wanted. Relief.

Mom snapped me back to reality, asking, "Are you gonna take a zero somewhere or use up your chance?" It was the best I could do. In Yahtzee, chance is an open combination. The dice don't have to complete a pattern—just add the face value, make the best of an otherwise useless turn. That was exactly what I needed. I needed to get through that night, reach a new day, when I might hear from Blake.

My mom was trying to help me do just that, offering distraction, but I couldn't unload my fears on her. She knew too intimately the fears of widowed mothers, kids growing up fatherless. She was only twelve when her dad died. The water of my worries was too deep for her, the fears too immediate for her to bear. And there were things she couldn't understand because her concern was once removed. She cared about Blake, but we'd only been married a few months. I was her daughter, George her grandson. We were her primary concern. She'd be just as mad at Blake as I was, if not more, if she knew he hadn't called in two weeks. She'd comfort me, sympathize with me, but she might not sympathize with Blake. It would be like those awful conversations when acquaintances asked nonchalantly if I'd talked to Blake lately and I would lie and say yes, just because it was easier. I accepted my mom's company, the buoys of board games and shopping trips she flung to keep me afloat, but I hid from her the reality of how close I felt to drowning, fearing I might pull her under with me. I needed a stronger swimmer to rescue me.

When then the phone rang, I turned instinctively to check the caller ID. It wasn't Blake. I knew it wouldn't be. But it was the next best thing. When I saw the local number, the name TJ's Tavern displayed beneath it, I immediately pictured Brock, bellied up to the bar with his dad, down the street from my parents' house. I jumped up to answer, knowing that this call offered the relief—the strong swimmer—I needed.

Ironically, all through childhood, Brock represented everything I feared about swimming. He was a townie with skin darkened from days at the pool, hair bleached so white in the sun that it eventually turned green with chlorine. He was one of the boys who could swim across the pool in a single breath, who made sport of dunking weaker swimmers like me—farm kids, who only came to the pool evenings, after milking cows and finishing chores. But by high school, Brock had stopped dunking me, stopped stealing my Sunday School offering, and become one of my best friends. Now, he was my lifeline. As Blake's oldest brother, he understood what it was like to love Blake dearly but be endlessly frustrated by him. As a soldier who had also been deployed to Iraq, Brock understood Blake in ways I couldn't. And now Brock was, like me, playing the support role. Stateside. Waiting for our soldier to return. He'd told me that once, after hearing news reports of American soldiers found, dismembered, in Afghanistan, he'd dreamed of some guy cutting his brother's leg off. He understood every side of both of our stories.

I could almost smell the Old Mil Light on his breath as Brock greeted me over the phone. "So, Amber, I was just sitting here wondering what're you doing tonight?"

Afraid my answer would sound too eager, I hesitated, but Brock continued.

"'Cause me and dad have been telling stories about Blake—that jerk—and we miss him." His voice was slurred, his words sincere. "And then I realize that if I miss his dumb ass this much, I can't imagine how much you do. How much you miss him. So . . ." Brock's voice trailed off for a moment. "Do you wanna come have a beer?"

I exhaled, "That would be great."

I hung up and turned to my mom, grabbing a fleece from the back of my chair as I said, "George is asleep, so if it's OK with you I'm gonna go talk to Brock for a while. You can call if you need anything." She nodded, but before she could answer, I heard the rumble of Brock's diesel truck in the driveway. I sighed a thank you as I rushed out the door.

When I pulled back the passenger door and prepared to step up onto the running board, I heard the fizzing pop of a beer cap releasing and saw Brock's hand stretched in my direction, offering me an Old Mil Light. We drove around for hours that night, down narrow dirt roads between ditches coated with thin, dirty snow and remnants of dry crab grass, listening to all our favorite songs and telling stories about Blake. His buck fever and his reputation for shooting deer in the ear, his aptitude as a batting practice pitcher, the time he tried to throw an alternator through a window but it bounced back. We sang every word of "Desperado" and "Tracks of My Tears," dedicating them to Blake, but when we came to "Midnight Train to Georgia," it just wasn't the same with Gladys Knight and only one Pip, so we gave up singing for talking.

"I hate to ask," Brock said. "But have you talked to dumb ass lately?"

I fiddled with change and shot gun shells in the console between us as I shook my head no. "Almost two weeks."

"Two weeks?" Brock popped open another beer. "That jerk. You know he could call you every day."

I was glad he shared my fury. "But this is Blake we're talking about," I said, giving him a break. "I know who I married."

"Yeah," Brock said, rolling his eyes, "I know the guy, too, and you're right, but it's still not fair."

"Maybe not," I said, working my fingernail under the label of my beer bottle. "But it's not like talking every day would help. He spends the whole time trying not to tell me anything about what's going on over there. I spend the whole time trying to tell him stories about George, stories I already wrote in letters, stories I already told him. It always feels weird."

"Yeah," Brock fixed his eyes on the gravel road ahead of him. "I remember calling home was a double-edged sword. I wanted to hear someone's voice, but then when I did it just made it harder to not be there." His chest swelled as he pulled in a long drag of smoke, which he exhaled slowly as he said, "I didn't even have a kid to think about. All I had to miss was hunting, baseball, and beer."

I turned in my seat so I could see Brock's profile and said what I'd been needing to say. "It's just so weird, because it seems like I'm always saying, 'I know there's something else I was going to tell you,' because I'm his wife and it seems like I should have important things to say." I continued to work the edged of my beer label free. "And then I tell him a story about George that I think he's going to love, and sometimes I can tell he doesn't get it. Like he has no idea how amazing it is to watch George smile at his own reflection in the mirror, has no idea what a big deal that is." I glanced at Brock to see if I'd shared too much. He squinted at the road ahead, listening intently. "I just want to cry sometimes, because Blake doesn't know what my life is like, how much I've changed now that I'm a mom, and I don't understand his, either."

The label of my beer loosened now, I pulled it off in one satisfying sheet, rolled it into a tight cylinder, lifted it to my lips like a cigarette. "Sometimes I'm afraid that when he comes home, he'll be different. That I won't know him anymore."

Brock answered quickly, cigarette dangling from his lips. "No, that's not . . . " He glanced at me, "It's not going to be like that. I can't say he won't have changed some, but he'll still be Blake."

I scraped at the gluey film left where my beer label used to be. I rolled the cold, wet mess into a tight ball, flung it on the dusty floor mat. "Yeah. I guess you're right." I began to relax, feeling water dispersing, air in my lungs pulling me upward. "Because, you know what the best part about talking to him is? Even in the really bad conversations when I can't think of anything to say, sometimes he laughs. A real laugh, one that just spills out." I smiled. "Then I know it's still him, and I think everything *will* be OK."

A few minutes later, when I stepped from Brock's truck onto my parents' driveway, I felt light. I skated over icy pavement. When I reached the garage, I steadied myself on the doorknob, and even though I knew Brock wouldn't see me, I turned back and waved as he rumbled onto the street.

Once inside, I knew I should shower and get some rest before George woke up, but I couldn't bring myself to wash off the smell of cigarettes that reminded me of Blake. As I drifted off to sleep in a recliner in front of the TV, I rested my cheek against my smoky fleece and, through the window, watched snowflakes fall against the bright glow of streetlights. This sign of winter, of seasons progressing, of time passing, gave me hope. I could survive the winter of Blake's deployment. Homesteaders had survived harsh winters on the South Dakota prairie and, over time, established shelterbelts to protect their farms from harsh winds. Blake and I had had little time to establish our own roots, but we lived among the shelter of family.

LESS THAN A WEEK BEFORE CHRISTMAS, I sat in my apartment copying phone numbers and addresses of potential caregivers I intended to follow up with as I made my final decision about daycare for George. I'd spent that morning at work, met the woman who'd been filling in for me, and worked out the details of a job-sharing agreement that would allow me to return part time in January. The idea of returning to work made me both nervous and excited. I missed the children and families I worked with, and I knew a routine would be good for me. My boss and co-workers were supportive, allowing me to ease back into work and ease George into a new routine of a few hours of daycare each day. But it was nerve wracking, choosing which strangers I would entrust with the care of my child. I labored over my list, adding weekly prices, notes about the pros and cons of in-home daycare and larger daycare settings. But all my planning suddenly took a backseat when Blake called. I'd barely smiled a hello when he hit me with the news: "I'm in Dallas."

"You're what?"

"I'm in Dallas, I should get to Sioux Falls in a few hours."

"You're coming home?" I laughed. "Well, you're in luck, I guess. I'm in Sioux Falls already." I shook my head in disbelief. "But seriously, you couldn't have given me a little more lead time?"

Now it was Blake who laughed. "Not on Army time. When they say it's time to go, it's time to go. I seriously didn't know until today, and then it was like, 'Go to the airport, and get on this plane.'"

I wasn't sure if I believed him, but I smiled as I said, "I'll be there waiting."

At the airport, I placed George's car seat near the bottom of the escalator and paced circles around it. Blake was easy to spot in his uniform, of course, but as the escalator carried him toward me, he seemed to become less familiar the closer he got—skinnier, which made him look older, somehow, when juxtaposed with the youthful backpack slung over his shoulder. He seemed swallowed up by his uniform, hidden beneath the short bill of the ACU cap that framed his face. When he was close enough to reach, I hugged him, but he slipped away, making a quick move toward the door. "Where'd you park?" he asked, racing forward.

Outside, I pointed to a back corner of the lot as I reminded Blake, "No more Ranger—we drive a family car now." He nodded, striding ahead as if he knew what he was looking for. I was stunned by this fast-motion reunion, struggling to keep pace with Blake. When I spotted the tan Impala, I balanced George's car seat against my hip and motioned with my free hand. "There it is." Blake glanced back to read my gesture and noticed my heavy load.

"I'm sorry. I should carry that," he offered, pausing to wait for me. It was a relief to be noticed. When Blake lifted the car seat from my arm, he groaned. "That's a good workout. You must be getting pretty buff, lugging this thing around."

As I pulled the keys from my pocket and fumbled to unlock the doors, I laughed. "Buff arms, sore back." Blake opened the rear door and placed George's car seat on the upholstery, deferring to me. I showed him how to click the seat into its base, then, as I closed the door, I held the keys out to him. "Why don't you drive?" Blake suggested. "I'm a little out of practice."

"Of course," I agreed. It was my car, after all. He'd never driven it before. And he was probably tired from traveling, more used to the rattle of a Humvee than the quiet ride of a four-door sedan. "Do you want to get something to eat?" I offered. "Stop anywhere? The apartment, maybe?"

"I guess I thought we'd get out of town, get to Bryant as fast as we can." His eagerness bubbled up again, his knee bobbing in the passenger seat. When I squinted at him as if to ask, Are you sure? What's the hurry? He explained, "I mean, I'd rather not stop. I'll just change when we get there."

It suddenly made sense. The brief hug. The near sprint to the door without so much as a glance in the car seat at our sleeping son. I remembered Guard drill weekends, how Blake avoided getting gas in his uniform. He didn't like having eyes on him. So, we made our way to Bryant, where he could change and settle into the comforts of home.

At his dad's house, Blake plucked George from his car seat and held him for the first time, marveling at how tiny he felt, even though to me the pounds he'd put on in the first months of life made him seem enormous compared to the tiny bread loaf I'd carried home from the hospital. Blake settled quickly into fatherhood, snuggling George back to sleep after a feeding. We spent two weeks driving around, drinking Old Mil Light, hanging out in his dad's garage, enjoying two Sunday dinners at Grandma Marilyn's, four Christmas parties with various family contingencies. Blake balanced the familiar with the new—a Baptism, learning to hold George's head while patting his back to coax out a burp, and co-sleeping with a two-month-old baby.

The weeks passed quickly, a blur that I remember primarily in photos. Four generations of Jensen men posing in front of a Christmas tree. Blake holding George in front of him, where bootied feet just reached his thighs, cooing, "You're a good stander, aren't you? You're a strong little guy." Our first family photo, George sporting his little coon outfit, as Blake called it—a Gymboree ensemble complete with thick-wale corduroy pants, a long-sleeved onesie and thick tan socks with raccoon heads printed on the toes.

The outfit reminded Blake of his own childhood, hunting coons with his dad and brothers, adopting orphaned babies as pets. The memory prompted him to sooth George with gurgling coon calls. It all felt comfortable. Normal. Easy. We enjoyed what we had while we had it. In the throes of winter, the early months of deployment, experiences were seeds, spread over the soil, potential, waiting to take root, promises of the family life that would come, eventually, but lying dormant until conditions were optimal, and they could sprout, take root, and flourish.

It was early morning in early January when Blake and I returned to the Sioux Falls airport, settling into the black upholstered chairs beneath an oversized bronze statue of former fighter pilot and ex-governor of South Dakota, Joe Foss. As I eased George from his car seat, I glanced over my shoulder, asking Blake, "Do you want to hold him?"

"Sure," he said. The stiff camouflage fabric of his uniform brushed my arm as I handed him our son, snuggled in soft fleece. Blake peered into George's face, squinting, not speaking. His lips curled into a soft smile.

Then, suddenly, abruptly, he turned away, inhaled a sharp breath, and stood in a business-like way. "OK," he said, handing George to me like a bag of groceries. He looked away and smoothed his pants with his palms. "Time to start heading up there. I better go, catch my flight."

I was stunned. Logically—intellectually—I understood the transformation I was witnessing. Blake had flipped the switch, stopping the emotional current of fatherhood from spilling over into the life he was returning to, the life of a soldier in Iraq. Some part of me knew this would happen. Still, I wasn't prepared for the abruptness. I dropped George in his car seat on top of buckles and straps, turned, and clung to my husband, trying to draw him back. I'd always thought Blake looked tall in his uniform, but as I stretched my arms over his shoulders, he felt almost out of reach.

His flight didn't leave for another half hour. *You can stay longer*, I begged him silently, pulling him towards me. Then I surrendered. *Let him go*, I told myself. *You want him to stay, but he can't.*

Blake paused to hug me one more time, whispering his mantra, "Everything will be all right." Then I watched him glide up the escalator, hoping he would turn back and wave, knowing that he wouldn't.

I COULDN'T HAVE PREDICTED in December that I, too, would become numb to the dull ache of absence, learn to detach, to live through, and even forget about the pain. But I did. I returned to work. George settled into his daycare routine, and the next five months passed relatively quickly, almost uneventfully. Until May, when Blake and the 147th Field Artillery experienced another tragedy. Gregory Wagner was killed when an IED struck his vehicle. The news was devastating, and I'm sure Blake called to tell me about it. But what I remember more than the conversation was the way Blake retreated into silence, his calls becoming gradually less frequent over the summer. I busied myself, followed Blake's brothers to Bryant Bucs baseball games, spent afternoons at my sister's lake house, and hours swinging at parks with George. Deciding I needed a change from the emotionally demanding job

I loved, I'd applied to graduate school at my alma mater, South Dakota State University, and once accepted began house hunting in Brookings. Blake supported the decision, preferring to live closer to home once he returned, and since Brock had returned to SDSU, too, to study civil engineering, we decided to look for a house we could all share once the school year began. With Blake's return only months away, we planned tentatively for the future.

One day toward the end of August, I curled into the third seat of my mom's suburban after an end-of-summer outing to Storybook Land in Aberdeen, South Dakota, home of L. Frank Baum, author of *The Wonderful Wizard of Oz*. We'd spent the day posing for pictures with Santa, the seven dwarfs, and Goldilocks, rode a magic carousel, walked through the enchanted forest and down the yellow brick road. As we made our way home, George and his cousins wilted into sleep in their car seats. My mom and sister chatted in the front seat, while I rested in the back, leather sticking to my skin, still rosy from sun, damp with sunscreen and sweat. I breathed slowly, nearing sleep, when suddenly I thought of Blake. It wasn't a gentle, pleasant memory that coaxed a smile from me, but a sudden remembering that jolted me awake.

It was the first time I had thought of him that day.

The sun was already dipping below the horizon of green, un-harvested cornfields before I finally thought about my husband, about how long it had been since I talked to him, about how long it might be before he'd be home from Iraq.

I sank lower in the seat, closed my eyes, and tried to find him, tried to transplant myself to another place where I could feel his presence. I imagined the dusty haze that lifted from the upholstery of his dad's truck and found myself thirsty for the penetrating smell of smoke. I tried to drink it in, curling my fingers near my lips, imagining the smoldering taste of Blake's skin, yellowed with the heat of cigarettes. I closed my eyes to inhale the smell of his uniform after a weekend of smoke breaks at drill, but my lungs filled with the disappointing chill of air-conditioning. I wanted to be somewhere with him—in the dugout after a baseball game, holding a beer and huddling against him for warmth. I tried to summon him, but I couldn't.

And so, I found my niece's travel desk, unrolled white paper from the pink plastic scroll, and began to write a letter I would never send. After a year's worth of words chosen carefully to convey how much I missed him, how much I hated living without him, how much better life would be when he returned, I bounced over the broken pavement of Highway 25 and wrote:

Dear Blake,

I almost forgot to miss you today.

My stomach lifted to my throat as I realized that Blake had become something far off. Something unpredictable. He had dissipated, slithered into the air in winding wafts of smoke. He had dissolved into memory and the dream of what a husband might be. In a month, he would begin his journey home from Iraq, but at that moment, he was still drifting. I wanted to let go of the possibility of losing him, to start imagining what life would be like once he was home. But I couldn't trust it. Not until he was actually there with me. So, I hung somewhere between anxiety and relief, suspended between consciousness and sleep, numbness and feeling.

It felt somehow like the epidural I'd received almost a year earlier when George was born, like being awake and aware, but feeling disconnected. I remembered the hospital, how convinced I'd been that I still had feeling in my legs, that when they started the operation, pain would slice through me. And I remembered my disbelief when I didn't feel anything. The slicing of skin registered as only a tickle, pulling and stretching as a slight sense of pressure, but really there was nothing. A void of sensation. That was how it felt, forgetting to miss Blake even though I missed him more than I'd ever realized I could. I knew he was out there, but I couldn't exactly feel him anymore.

I didn't finish the letter I would never send. But if I had, I would have explained the sensation. I would have written:

That's how I feel about forgetting to miss you, Blake. It's a sort of suffering that I've come to expect to sweep over me several times a day—when the sound of George's rasping snore flashes me an image of you, pitching baseballs to a toddler you never rocked to sleep as a baby; when I watch TV and try to snuggle into the arm of the couch, wishing that arm would wrap itself around me, extend a soft-skinned hand to trace circles on my shoulder until it burns on my freckled skin—and when it doesn't come, I feel numb. As if half of me has died. And I want to scream, but I can't, because that is when I realize that if something does happen, if you don't come home from war, life will go on.

If you don't come home, I imagine that for a while it would feel like part of me was missing. Not just as if I couldn't feel my legs, but as if they were actually gone and I were nothing more than a bust, a resin form of head, neck, and shoulders, sitting still and lifeless on the shelf of a library or an office somewhere, where people pass by, pretending not to see me, my testimony to death and tragedy. But eventually I would start to feel a prickling numbness, a dead-heavy foot, a phantom limb. And eventually that foot would twitch involuntarily, come back to life, remind me that I'm not completely broken, that I can still feel, move, live. Then I would reach down and tug on that lead foot, drag it around for a while, until it gave in and started to wiggle and flex, then finally function again.

So, I can't scream, because I know it is a good thing—the fact that I wouldn't die without you—but I hate it at the same time. I know you would want me to move on—maybe run into that guy I always flirted with in college, the one I bumped into the summer before we were married, the one who asked my uncle if I was still single just weeks before our wedding—but I don't want to have to. I'm afraid of the possibility of losing you, of having to live without you. But I'm sick with knowing that somehow, eventually, I could.

Can you understand the guilt of that?

And can you forgive me?

I hope so, because even now, as I realize that life could go on without you, I know that you are always part of me and that you always will be, even if it seems like I am forgetting. I still see you, feel you, around me whenever George's face transforms into yours with the furrow of his brow; whenever I enter a hazy bar, met someone's smoke circles on the street, or catch a whiff of burning autumn leaves; whenever the tinny, cheap twinge of Old Mil Light trickles from a sweating can to my lips, making me long to inhale the smoke of you.

Four

IT WAS A SCORCHING SUNDAY at the end of September when I stood in the parking lot of the Yankton Armory among a cluster of family. My parents, my son, Blake's dad and brothers, his grandparents, my brother and his family. At home, we all lived in a tight circle of extended family, most of us in a forty-mile radius of Bryant, but that day, we gathered in the midst of a larger family unit—Yankton's Battery C, 1st Battalion, 147th Field Artillery—itself much like one immediate family within the still larger, extended family of the South Dakota Army National Guard. Our group might have been the in-laws, connected, but on the periphery, because Blake was attached to the unit only for deployment. He'd never done weekend drills with these soldiers, and though I'd received notice of Family Readiness events in Yankton throughout the deployment, I'd never attended. We were separated from this family by a hundred and fifty miles, connected to them by deployment and now homecoming. Each report—"They've landed in Sioux Falls." "They're on the interstate." "Less than thirty miles away."—teased us with the possibility of tension relieved.

With George perched on my hip, his cheeks flushed deep pink, I bounced on the balls of my feet, regretting the heeled boots I'd worn in hopes that they might make me look slimmer, more like I had pre-deployment, pre-baby, more like the girl Blake had fallen in love with. I straightened my posture and sucked in my stomach. My own cheeks flushed as I anticipated reconnecting with the shy athlete I fell in love with, welcoming home my soldier, and watching him transform into loving husband and father. My eyes, thirsty for the sight of him, scanned the horizon. Heat radiated from pavement, blurring white highway lines. I nuzzled George's cheek, whispering, "Daddy will be here any minute. Your daddy's almost home!"

Of course, I knew that George couldn't comprehend the words, in spite of my efforts to plant them in his vocabulary. After Blake's two-week R&R, I had printed a picture of him, zooming in on our family photo from George's baptism, blowing up Blake's smiling face so large that the image came out grainy. I dangled it from a string of plastic rings on the handle of George's car seat, so that he would see it wherever we went. I'd filled a padded plastic book titled "Who loves baby?" with pictures of grandparents, uncles, cousins, and that same family photo, full frame. When we flipped through the book, I paused dramatically before the last page, then turned it and exclaimed, "Daddy!" with a burst of excitement that I hoped was endearing, not jack-in-the-box frightening. George heard the word enough to recognize it, but I knew there was a possibility that he would be scared of his dad. He was a cautious child. When encountering strangers, he studied their expressions and my reactions, his brow furrowed, sometimes for twenty minutes before he relaxed into a smile. But George had always connected with my dad, Blake's dad, and Blake's brothers, reaching for their stubbled faces and questioning them with raised eyebrows, and I hoped this prepared him to welcome another deep-voiced man into his life. So, as we waited, I repeated the words, the names for this man George was about to meet, priming him. "Almost home, George—Dad's almost here."

A buzzing swelled amidst the crowd as a caravan of vehicles came into view, a dotted line growing on the horizon. I squeezed George and rubbed my hand frenetically over his back. I pointed and whispered, "There he is!" George's gaze followed my outstretched hand. Seeing nothing but a crowd of strangers, he leaned into me. I bobbed him gently, kissed his warm cheek.

When the trio of gleaming black buses pulled into the parking lot, forming a barricade between us and the highway, cheers erupted. The busses, with pastel banners painted along their sides, looked like the ones I'd ridden when I'd toured Mexican beaches and mountain villages—simple charter busses, not the Humvees and artillery trucks I'd envisioned. When a door coughed open and the first uniformed man descended the stairs, expectations scattered. Chaos ensued.

Families rushed forward. Stairs rattled as soldier after soldier stepped down. Each of them looked different—a sharp-chinned teenager, a flat face perforated with narrow eyes, a round face framed by bushy brows—but the same, too—clean shaven, ears exposed beneath thin-billed, camo hats. But none looked like Blake. I panicked.

My scanning became frantic. I searched for his familiar, plump cheeks, cut deep with dimples, his narrow squinting eyes disappearing in a smile. I wondered had Blake shaved the mustache his buddies had goaded him into growing? Had he lost even more weight than when he was home for R&R eight months earlier? Was everyone off the bus? Why couldn't I find him?

My body tingled. I was failing.

This was supposed to be the magical part of our story. We should have been drawn together through the crowd like magnets. Something was wrong. Without the sight of Blake to anchor my thoughts, my mind spiraled to the worst possible, least likely, conclusion. What if he's not here? A logical impossibility. They hadn't seen combat for weeks. There was de-mobilization in Kuwait, the checking of inventory, the change of command, overseas and cross-country travel. He had called to tell me when he'd arrive home. There was absolutely no way that Blake wasn't there, but I couldn't find him. Logic gave way to irrational certainty.

I reached across my body to hold George steady, pull him closer. My voice quivered, "Do you see your daddy?" I hunched my neck, lowering my forehead to meet George's, and squinted to feign excitement. "He's here somewhere, buddy. Let's go see." I scanned the crowd again.

Then, through the flap of flags, glare of sun off busses, and circles of people holding tight to one another, I caught a glimpse of Blake—all cheeks and wide grin, eyes framed by smile lines— almost within reach. He walked in our direction, infuriatingly patient, as always. I couldn't wait. I wedged my right shoulder between bodies, shielding George from the crowd, as I angled my way toward him. I cast my hand up over a barrier of strangers and let it fall, catching the base of Blake's clean-shaven chin. I reeled him in. Bodies pushed and pulled around us, so when the crowd parted slightly, my feet stuttered, and I collapsed into Blake, who steadied me. His hands clasped tightly behind my back, like our first dance, our first kiss under a cottonwood tree. My forehead met his smooth cheek. I felt his smile.

With George sandwiched in between, our bodies fit together. Blake pulled back, peering over his wire-rimmed frames at George, presenting a thin finger, which George clasped with his chubby hand. "Nice to meet you, young man," Blake cooed. George responded with a tired, heat-glazed stare, but he didn't pull away. I rested my head on Blake's shoulder, absorbing the radiance of the moment, as he grinned. "Yes, it's very nice to meet you."

We made our way back to the cluster of family, where Midwestern men who never hug, hugged, arms clapping around backs. Blake's grandparents waited their turn, grandmothers first, balancing on tiptoes as they reached up to embrace him. Grandpas, next, clasped hands and patted his shoulder before, finally, a brief embrace. My mom offered a side hug, my niece a timid leaning hug from her place in my dad's arms. My dad reached out his hand, said, "Good to have you home."

At the center of our circle, George, dressed in copper canvas overalls that I'd chosen because they reminded me of the Carhartt's Blake wore for hunting, extended a hand to his dad, offering the stuffed baseball he'd held all morning. When Blake smiled and reached out, George's chubby fingers unclenched, dropping the ball. Blake raised his eyebrows and gasped, "Uh oh."

Blake peered over his glasses, eyes wide with exaggerated surprise. He leaned close to George, and teased, "All gone." Then, he stooped to pick up the ball. When Blake stood, red-stitched leather in hand, exclaiming, "There it is!" George reached for him. The game of disappearing and reappearing seemed apt.

As the game gave way to small talk, Blake held George out in front of him, testing his weight. Turning to me, he asked, "What is he, about twenty pounds?"

"Nineteen and a half," I teased. "He was just at the doctor last week." I smiled at Blake's accuracy, a sure sign that he was tuned-in, ready for fatherhood.

Ready as we were to move on to family life and home, military ceremony held us in place. After a parade through Yankton, we arrived at the auditorium for a deactivation ceremony—our final obligation. As we made our way into the building, voices and bodies ricocheted off cinderblock walls. I moved sideways through the crowd, clinging to Blake to avoid being swallowed up in the euphoric sea of friends and family. Between bodies, I glimpsed a display of helmets, rifles, and boots. In our frenzied shuffle, I hurried past without registering meaning, but the image etched itself in my mind, solid and significant.

Inside, bleachers groaned beneath the weight of a shoulder-to-shoulder crowd. Blake led us to a row of folding chairs, where he sat down, perching George on his lap. As sweat trickled down my back, I slipped an arm behind him, resting it on the cool metal back of his chair. Bodies filled seats around us.

When voices hushed, I lifted my gaze to the stage set up a few rows ahead of us, expecting to see a speaker at the podium. I was surprised to find the stage still empty. Then the legs of a folding chair screeched behind us. I startled. When I heard what sounded like a muffled yell, I kept my head tuned forward, afraid to acknowledge the sound. The auditorium grew still. When another shout broke the silence, I traced it to a man, standing at floor level in front of the stage, facing the crowd of uniformed soldiers. Another folding chair screeched, another voice called out, this time an audible, "Sir, yes sir." Then silence again. The next time the voice ahead of me boomed, I recognized what he called out as a name. This time I anticipated a soldier's response, the silence that would follow. I settled into the cadence of this military roll call, noticing the character of each soldier's response, some soft staccato, others booming vowels punctuated with a deep "Hoo-ah." The names didn't register, only pattern, sound. And then, suddenly, silence came in the wrong place.

A name called. No squeaking chair. No shouted response.

When the name was called a second time, I held my breath, hoping for an answer. It didn't come. I wondered what kind of trouble this soldier might be in, what the repercussions might be for skipping out on this ceremony. But then the roll call resumed, marching steadily, alphabetically, approaching Jensen. Blake slid George onto my lap. At the sound of his name, Blake responded firmly and stood at attention. I shifted George's weight, allowing the heat of his body and the rhythm of ceremony to lull me into what felt almost like sleep. Until the pattern was broken again.

Name. No response. Silence.

Repeat.

This time, the silence created space for understanding, connecting with the image of helmets, boots, and rifles in the hallway. The soldier's cross. I realized there would be two more names called with no response. These were the names of men who could not answer: Daniel Chuka, Allan Kokesh, Richard Schild, Gregory Wagner. Casualties of war. My jaw clenched, tears collected, as I confronted the shameful privilege of forgetting.

As the roll call ended and the soldiers around us took their seats, Blake lifted George from my lap. Exhausted, I let my gaze fall, landing on the eyeleted bottom half of Blake's bootlaces, following them up to the hooked upper half. I imagined families who longed for soldiers' boots to be filled. I imagined the parade that should have welcomed home their sons, husbands, fathers winding past their houses. I wondered what this day felt like for them, if they stepped out into their yards, if they could bring themselves to be happy for us.

I glanced up to find George—cheeks red, mouth relaxed, eyelids heavy—slouched into his father. Blake stroked the side of his cleanly shaven chin against the hot, damp, hair of his sleeping son. A relieved sigh relaxed my shoulders and rounded my back as I realized, those families would want this for us.

I closed my eyes and leaned into Blake, fitting my head into the hollow crook of his neck. I slowed my anxious breathing to match the steady rhythm of his breaths.

OUTSIDE THE AUDITORIUM, everything inched towards evening. The sun glowed above the horizon but below the rim of the immense building, so we lingered—hundreds of us—in the shade of the auditorium, breathing in the crisp air of a South Dakota evening in September, when summer recedes slowly, its warmth and life and shades of green lingering, but giving way gradually to autumn's cooler evenings and muted earthy pallet. The buzz of voices dulled to a hum, everyone settling in, spreading out.

Our progress in the direction of the parking lot was slow, stalling each time a segment of our group pulled away in the direction of their car with a few words, a quick hug, and eventually movement again. Urgency subsided. We were headed in the right direction, headed toward home. As a breeze shivered over my sweat-dried skin, I linked my arm with Blake's. I savored the cool air after suffocating heat.

But as we picked up our stride, nearing our final stalling point, the final separation of our group—my parents from Blake's dad and brothers—synchronicity failed. While I followed my parent's lead toward their suburban straight ahead, Blake veered left, toward his dad's truck. Our bodies pulled in opposite directions. I shifted George from my right hip to the left, tilting my head in the direction of my parents' car. "His seat's in there." I lifted my hip, offering George's body to Blake. "If you take him, I can grab it."

Blake shook his head. "That's OK, I'm sure it'll be fine."

I titled my head and squinted in Blake's direction. Surely he didn't mean George would be fine without a car seat. I fumbled, "Well, yeah, but I can just grab it. It's no big deal."

With my free hand, I drew George's cheek to my shoulder, snuggling my cheek to his temple protectively, kissing the soft top of his head as Blake clarified, "He can just ride with them."

My shoulders buckled. I spoke slowly. The vision of a quiet

car ride, with Blake studying the sleeping face of his son as we held hands over the seat behind him, dismantled as I pieced together this new possibility. "So, you want to ride with your dad, but you want George to ride with my parents."

Blake nodded. "There isn't room. They all rode together."

They meant Blake's dad, two of his brothers, and one future sister-in-law. So, it was true, there would barely be room in the truck for Blake and I, much less George and his car seat. Disappointment clouded logic. Blake was coming home to *his* family. His dad. His brothers. Not *ours*. Not father and son. Husband and wife. I blinked at the realization.

On the one hand, it made sense. Blake had a lifetime of connection to them. They had a year's worth of hunting and baseball stories to catch up on. If my parents and I tried to ask about Blake's year in Iraq, our questions would come from outside the military experience and might feel like an inquisition, not the understanding exchange that would come with Brock and Brad, both deployed a year earlier. The leather seats of my parents' suburban would feel foreign, not filled with the familiar smell of farm dust and cigarette smoke. Blake was returning to a world transformed—a world he had only read about in letters, seen glimpses of during his few days at home, and studied in the single-dimension of photos. Maybe he needed to ease into that new world, situate himself in the familiar before being bombarded with dirty diapers, desperate searches for pacifiers, and naptime routines.

But I couldn't help but wonder. Was this what detachment looked liked? Blake had already missed a year's worth of coos and giggles and smiles. How could he stand to miss even an hour more?

I glanced in the direction of my parents' suburban, the windows my niece had painted with red, white, and blue stars, and then back at Blake. He nodded slightly, encouragingly, patient but resolved. "It'll be fine," he said with a gentle smile. I relented.

Blake lingered between rows of parked cars while I walked to my parents' car and snapped George into his car seat. I tried to nonchalantly dismiss my mom's confusion, saying, "We're just gonna ride with them." I couldn't look her in the eye, for fear that I might cry. My dad came around to the passenger side, resting his hand on the open door while I tucked George's satin blanket around him and kissed his forehead. When I stepped down, my dad closed the door and placed his immense hands on my shoulders. His strong arms tethered me like cables training a leaning young tree. "We'll do fine, Ber. Enjoy yourselves and take as long as you want." When my dad pulled me in to his thick frame, tears came. "It's just tonight. George will be sleeping before we pull out of the parking lot. It'll all look different in the morning."

I leaned into him for a moment, letting my expectations crumble against him, then stood, blinked away tears, and thanked him. When I reached Blake, we weaved our way across the parking lot, dotted with cars. I linked my arm with his, again.

The Jensens were settled into the truck when Blake and I climbed in. I welcomed the tight fit of four in the back seat, the way my shoulder overlapped Blake's and I could lean into him. We joked about stopping at Bonanza, which used to be the fanciest restaurant any of us could imagine, with its enticing pictures of char-marked proteins, its stainless-steel lined plates and endless salad bar, but we agreed wordlessly on what we were really hungry for: the protected solitude of the truck, familiar stories and laughter. We headed north on Highway 81, and as soon as we passed city limits, Brock asked me to slide open the window behind me and grab a twelve pack.

When I try to remember that drive, all that comes to me is feeling. Warm cheeks and close bodies. Cold beer. Laughter loosening tense muscles. I can imagine the stories we might have told of Blake's Legion baseball legends, the recap of the season Blake had missed, the team party where George gummed the lip of an Old Mil Light can. It all feels comfortable, like the quilts my grandmothers stitched, thin but weighty, warming but cool to the touch, everything smooth and fluid, including Brock's questions about Iraq, and the way the brothers sized up similarities and differences between their deployments. When I called to check on George, Mom assured me he was sleeping and said she'd call if she needed anything. I settled back into the familiar cadence of story and laughter, savoring the history of us, how much of our story was represented there in that truck. As that history, the elation of the day, and the tinny taste of beer loosened the stronghold of expectation, I realized Blake had been right. We needed this ride home together. This was an important part of us.

Two hours later, as we neared Bryant, I had to pee so bad I worried I might not make it. Wetting my pants didn't seem like the most flattering welcome home image, and when the men stopped to "check the tires," I almost took to the ditch to squat amongst the tall grass, but we were at the four-mile corner, so I thought I could make it. But then, I overheard Brock's phone call to the owner of the local bar who also happened to be a volunteer fireman. "We're at the four-mile corner," Brock said. "Are you guys ready? Or should we cruise for a few minutes and circle back here to meet you?" He grinned as he said, "OK, we'll just wait." Within moments, just as Blake prepared to settle back into the seat next to me, sirens and lights appeared on the horizon.

"You're kidding me," Blake laughed, his mouth falling open. "This is too much," his voice boomed. "Too much." He was visibly flattered but embarrassed at the thought of this small-town welcome home parade.

As the fire truck rolled to a stop, Blake opened his door. I placed my hand on his knee and leaned into whisper, "I don't think I can ride on the back of that truck. I really have to pee." I looked him in the eye. "I'm sorry."

Blake jumped down, boots crunching gravel as he landed on the shoulder of the road. "Don't worry," he said. "We'll just meet up at the bar." The bar. I hadn't thought about the bar, but of course the fire truck parade would end at the bar. This was going to take longer than I'd expected. He kissed me and hurried off.

As the men climbed onto the back of the fire truck, Liza jumped into the driver's seat of the pickup and asked, "What? You're not up for another parade?"

When I explained how badly I needed a bathroom, she graciously drove me straight to TJ's Tavern, dropping me off at the door before driving away in search of a parking spot on the packed Main Street. Entering the bar, I marveled at the wall-to-wall crowd, on par with the opening weekend of pheasant hunting season and the annual Fourth of July street dance. I weaved my way to the restroom, waving off bottles of beer on the way, shouting, "I'll be right back," over the din of the crowd. When I emerged, the fire truck was pulling to a stop outside, its sirens announcing Blake's arrival. I found a place against the back wall where I could see the front entrance and waited for the doors to swing open.

A cheer erupted as Blake was swallowed up by a sea of friends and neighbors, his head bobbing, becoming visible for a moment between handshakes and slaps on the back, then disappearing again as he dipped down into a hug or leaned into a conversation. With each glimpse of Blake's wide grin, I smiled, too, watching as he made his way in my direction. He was enjoying his moment but making his way back to me. He was at home. Completely relaxed. And I was happy, my cheeks warm from the beer and the thrill of watching Blake at ease. Movements and laughter were synchronized, the circles of one brown bottle overlapping the circle left behind on the bar by its predecessor, as rounds of drinks were ordered so fast that it was impossible to keep track of where each came from.

When someone slid a shot glass down the bar in Blake's direction, I cringed, but Blake pushed it away. "I've got a wife and a kid. I'm a grown up now. I don't have to do shots." He laughed. "That's why you have kids, so you can say, 'nope, gotta get home.'" He looked at me and started in on a comically dramatic, sidestepping, finger-snapping, *West Side Story* exit. I smiled with relief.

As we made our way toward the door, Blake paused at the offer of another round—he could never pass by without conversation much less turn down a beer from Roger Davidson—but then he gave me a reassuring sideways glance and a couple finger snaps to show that he was just playing along. These signs of connection took the edge off the sting I'd felt earlier. Blake wanted this moment, his reunion with his family, and he would accept the recognition of the community, but he still wanted *us*. He thanked RD for the beer, lifting the bottles in his direction and giving him a nod, then nudged me forward. Before we slipped onto Main Street, Blake reached back inside and set two untouched bottles of Old Mil in front of the two patrons closest to the door.

It felt so good to step outside.

The street was quiet, the buzz of voices from inside barely audible. It was finally just the two of us.

Our fumbling walk down the street reminded me of our wedding night, the walk from our reception to our temporary honeymoon suite. But this time we walked toward a more certain future. Now, deployment was in the past. Blake was home. I almost wished we had more than a single block to walk to my parent's house, but the autumn chill cut through my cotton shirt. I leaned into Blake, partly for warmth, partly to stabilize him, but mostly just to be near him. I whispered, "I'm so glad you're home." He squeezed my shoulder, then halted for an abrupt kiss before leaning his forehead against mine, peering over his glasses as he smiled. "It's good to be home."

AT MY PARENTS' HOUSE, we fell quickly into relieved sleep in my old bedroom upstairs, but sometime during the night, the mattress shifted, and I woke. Ears trained by eleven months of motherhood, tuned to pick up the swish of sheets, and the whimper of an imminent cry, I lifted my head from the pillow, listening for George. Instead, I heard a desperate roar. The wail of an animal trapped or under attack, wanting to flee.

It seemed like it should have been a dream. I knew it wasn't.

Even in the blur of sleep, I knew Blake was there and knew this strange sound came from him. I knew my surroundings: a pink bedroom with sloped ceilings, one door leading to a bonus room over the garage, another leading to a miniature hallway, not tall enough to stand in, and one more leading to another hallway that wound around to a stairway and down to the main floor. Before I could make sense of the sound, my mind catalogued exit strategies.

I propped myself up on elbows to examine the room. Blake wasn't in bed beside me. I scanned the dark for the source of the wailing. Skin flashed near the edge of the bed in shadowed, thrashing movements. I heard another moaning wail, and the fine hairs on my neck and arms lifted. Before I could think, I reached out. My fingers grazed warm, smooth skin.

I felt at once pulled toward that warmth—my hand hovering, fingertips pulsing—and repelled by it. I pulled away from a creature I feared might turn on me, thrashing like a trapped animal and willing to gnaw its own limb off to gain freedom. How much more willing, I wondered, to lash out at me? As Blake wailed and scratched, my mind whirred. *What was he doing? What was he dreaming?* Before I could settle on any answers, Blake mumbled something, crouched beside the bed, and roared. His hands circled pink wallpaper, searching for something, then he began scratching, as if trying to gain traction, as if to scramble over something. I pictured the cinderblock walls surrounding homes in Mexico, shards of glass cemented to the top. It was all so disorienting. Alcohol still buzzed through my body. As my eyes adjusted to the darkness, as the reality around me became clearer instead of becoming more grounded, more firmly footed, I became more uncertain.

I slid off the bed and backed toward the door as if walking through shallow water, knowing the bottom could drop off suddenly. I tiptoed to what felt like a safe distance, then whispered, "Blake, are you OK?"

His scratching and wailing slowed, but he didn't acknowledge me. I stepped toward Blake, my body in a protective sideways stance, and reached out. My fingers grazed his skin. "Blake?" His hands, still on the wall, slowed. He mumbled something unintelligible but not unknowable, not threatening and sounded human again. My fear leveled. I laid my hand on his bare shoulder. He stiffened.

Then, suddenly, Blake brushed past me and out of the room. I heard the bathroom door swing open and close. A minute later, Blake returned, shuffled around the foot of the bed, and laid down, facing the wall. I positioned myself beside him, not sinking in toward the center of the mattress, not leaning into him, but balancing my body in a straight line near the edge of the mattress. I whispered, "Is everything OK?" He mumbled. I leaned in his direction, curled my knees up to my chest, and whispered, "You really scared me."

As Blake slipped back into sleep, I slipped from bed to turn on a hallway light, cracking the door to let a sliver in, then eased myself back onto the mattress. Still sleeping, Blake turned to face me. I studied his thick eyebrows, the narrow bridge of his nose, his wide, soft cheeks. I summoned memories of those cheeks dimpled with a smile, those eyebrows peaked playfully in debate. I reached out to clasp his hand and willed myself to trust the memory of his gentle touch, to forget this frenzied scratching. This was Blake. He would never hurt me. I turned my body and shimmied toward him, pulling his arm around my waist. When he laced his fingers with mine and pulled me closer, I exhaled my fears. Breathing carefully, purposefully, I told myself that, after fourteen months playing the role of Blake's something-to-come-home-to—a role I was powerless in, because my actions could never determine outcomes

—I could take comfort in his presence. He was here now. I could take action in this role. I couldn't be sure what the future would hold, but we would figure it out together. I could offer support, space, whatever Blake needed. In spite of uncertainty, in the comfort of connection, I found sleep.

When I woke, Blake lay beside me, breathing evenly. I studied his smooth skin, the sharp edge of his fine hair, close-shaven along his neck and behind his ears. Sunlight streamed in from the window. I rested my cheek against his smooth chest, ran my fingers over the curves and angles of his shoulder and collarbone. In the peace of that morning, the wailing and scratching of the night before seemed almost like a dream. I wanted to wake Blake to see if he remembered, or to ask if he'd had a bad dream, but I feared the answer. And I wanted to let him sleep. Still, I couldn't resist the urge to maximize the moment of connection. I sneaked downstairs to lift George, wrapped in his favorite blue satin blanket, from the crib in my parents' room, and returned to bed, where I lay my son beside my husband. I studied similarities. Sharp jaw contouring round cheeks. Shapely, pronounced lips. Eyes closed in thin dashes of sleep.

Eventually, Blake flipped onto his right side to face George and I. He blinked a few times, eyes skipping from side to side, assessing his surroundings, before he looked directly at me. Blake smiled, then rested his head back on the pillow and closed his eyes.

"Did you sleep OK?" I asked.

Adjusting his pillow, Blake answered, "Mmm hmm."

I studied his sleep-moistened eyelids. "Do you remember getting up to go to the bathroom?" When Blake answered with a guttural sound, shaking his head from side to side, I searched for a flicker of recognition, a twitch of his lip. Detecting nothing, I continued. "You made quite a bit of noise."

"That's weird," he said, this time opening his eyes, but not looking at me. He turned his head, eyes dancing. Did I imagine them moving back and forth over the low seam where wall met ceiling? Before I could be sure, Blake had readjusted his pillow and closed his eyes. "Nope, I don't remember anything," he said. "I slept great." And with that he closed the conversation I'd been hesitant to open. With George sleeping on the mattress between us, we retreated into silence and the slow waking of a Sunday morning with the potential of Blake's homecoming.

Five

THE DAY AFTER BLAKE'S HOMECOMING, after eating dinner at his Grandma Marilyn's, where his cousins greeted him with welcome home posters they had colored and peppered with images of flags and deer and cats, we finally made our way home—to our home, the duplex I had moved into in Brookings when I started graduate school the month before. It was already getting dark when we arrived, so as Blake unbuckled George from his car seat and I led him to the backdoor, I explained that he would have to swing the hinged doorknob up, not down like most doors. He laughed at the story of his younger brother, Brad, removing the doorknob to fit our washing machine in on moving day, then re-installing it upside down.

Blake had read about the duplex in letters and heard about it in phone calls, but as we made our way in together for the first time, I pointed out the places he should not step—the lose ceramic tile in the kitchen, the creaky spot in the wood floor outside the bathroom—and what to expect of bedtime routines—a warm bath, followed by three books, and back-scratching to lull George to sleep. I guided Blake to his side of the closet, his dresser beside the bed, and eventually, we settled in on the couch to watch TV.

As soon as we'd made ourselves at home, Brock arrived. In the months leading up to Blake's homecoming, as I searched for a place for our family to land in Brookings, Brock was also house hunting. I don't know if he had suggested it, or if it was Blake's idea, or mine, but somehow, we'd all agreed that if we found a three-bedroom place, Brock should live with us. I didn't know at the time that the living arrangement was Blake's way of paying Brock back the money he'd spotted him for my engagement ring, but our duplex included a basement with two bedrooms—one we'd use as an office, another for Brock—a bathroom, and a playroom, in addition to an unfinished space for storage and laundry. It seemed like a perfect fit, since Brock and I seemed to be following the same low-income, career-student trajectory. I was pursuing a Masters in English. Brock had completed law school, landed a job and passed the bar exam before his deployment to Iraq, but after his deployment, he decided criminal law wasn't his thing and returned to South Dakota State University to pursue a degree in civil engineering.

I suppose it could have seemed like an intrusion when Brock walked in on our first night at home as a family, but it didn't. He came to stand in the living room doorway, chatted for a few minutes about our week's schedule—he sometimes picked George up from daycare when I had evening class—and he offered Blake some TV recommendations, then he retreated to the basement. His presence felt familiar and comforting. Eventually, we would joke about the living situation, calling Brock George's weird uncle who lived in the basement. We would laugh at the irony of a bar-certified lawyer living, rent free, in a cinderblock basement with turf-quality carpet—the basement, nonetheless, of his under-employed, veteran brother and graduate-student sister-in-law. But Brock had been a best friend to both Blake and I for most of our lives. He understood us, and he understood what it meant to readjust to civilian life after a deployment. I felt a sense of security, believing that Brock might provide a bridge between the military and civilian sides of Blake's life, the past and future of our family.

Opportunities for adjustment and understanding continued when, just a few weeks later, Blake and I drove to Sioux Falls for an Army-sponsored, post-deployment, reintegration Family Retreat. Outside of the activation and deactivation ceremonies that bookended Blake's deployment, this was the first military event I'd attended with him and the first time he was reporting back to the National Guard for anything. Blake had adapted well to family life. He seemed at ease with days in a house full of toddler noise and toys, quiet nights at home after early bedtime. George seemed drawn to him, unquestioning, as if he had known all through that first year of his life that he had a dad who would be coming home. And when he wasn't playing the role of father, Blake seemed entirely unchanged. He spent daytime hours working part time with my dad and driving around with his family, scouting deer, evening hours perched in tree stands, his bow and arrow resting on his lap, and nighttime hours at our duplex, watching Adult Swim, the History Channel, and Food Network or HGTV. In our daily lives, it was easier to forget than to remember that he was a soldier. It seemed like a past tense part of his identity. But he was still enlisted in the South Dakota Army National Guard and planned to complete his twenty years of service, so I viewed this military event as a journey into his world.

The weather had veered sharply from the hot September Sunday when Blake returned home to the biting winds of fall turning winter. As we made our way into the convention center, I looked in Blake's direction, shielding my face from slicing wind and snowflakes. Blake warned, "This is gonna be ridiculous. I hate these Army things."

I quickened my step and zipped the collar of my down coat up to my neck, then tucked my gloved hand around Blake's arm. "It can't be that bad," I insisted. I was actually looking forward to the event. I expected to feel like an outsider—the Army wife who didn't understand military hierarchy or acronyms, the veteran's wife who had no more idea what her husband had seen, heard, or done in Baghdad than to say that he trained Iraqi policemen—but I welcomed the chance to learn. I thought a weekend with other soldiers and soldiers' wives might link military and married life. Maybe we'd become friends—these men who had served together in Iraq and wives who had endured a year of worry—and arrange double dates, share stories about the strain of long-distance relationships, the relief of being together again. I thought of the weekend as an extended date, just speeches in place of movies, pamphlets in place of menus. Really, I was excited just to spend the time with Blake.

When we entered the convention center, we were greeted by a string of tables clothed in navy blue, stainless steel serving plates half heaped with muffins, and covered dishes steaming with remnants of breakfast meats and scrambled eggs. The hallway was quiet. The only sign of people was the buzz of voices from a room halfway down the long corridor. "I guess we should get some food," Blake said, directing me toward the service line. We filled our plates and made our way to the room that hummed with voices and occasional bursts of laughter. As we entered, Blake scanned the white-clothed round tables, but before we could sit, a tall kid with full cheeks and a huge grin approached us, shouting, "Jensen!" and slapping Blake on the back. "So, this is the wife? Aren't you gonna introduce me?"

"Yeah," Blake laughed, motioning with his plate full of food. "Amber, this is Bryce. My gunner." I smiled, nodding slightly, and marveled at this rapid-fire introduction and the implied power and subordination. Blake's gunner. Bryce seemed genuinely excited to see Blake and eager to meet me. He reached for my hand. I set my plate on a table and accepted his handshake. "Your hubby had to put up with my shit the whole time. And I had to put up with him ordering me around. Your husband can be a real asshole." His friendliness put me at ease, and he surprised me, breaking my young-kid-who-just-wants-to-tell-drinking-stories assessment by asking, "How about the kid? How's George doing?"

Blake probably told him that George was great, probably mentioned something about his perfectly round head—the feature he liked most to describe—but as quickly as the connection manifested, Blake severed it. Instead of turning the conversation back to Bryce, he said, "Well, we're gonna grab a seat. It's really good to see you, Bryce. We'll probably catch up with you later."

Bryce slapped Blake on the back. "That's Jensen. All business-as-usual." He grinned and said, "We'll see you around." As he turned, Bryce was already shouting another soldier's name and reaching his hand out for another greeting.

Blake shook his head and smiled. "Ah, Bryce."

"One of your buddies?" I asked.

"Yeah, I guess so. He was the only guy that was with me the whole time. The rest of us got moved around, but Bryce was always in my truck. A good kid. Just a pup, really." Blake laughed. "Man, sometimes I wanted to wring his neck. But he's a good kid."

Picking up my plate, balancing coffee in my other hand, I weighed this image of Blake against his usual demeanor. A good kid. Just a pup, really. We'd been in the convention center all of ten minutes, and Blake had transformed into a father figure, or a big brother at least, to this boisterous kid. It made sense. I pictured Blake as a quiet, natural leader, someone people respected and felt drawn to. An image flashed in my mind of Blake leading the huddle in a football game. Calm, but assertive and clear. It was something I'd never witnessed up close, but I relished the insight.

Blake motioned with his plate to a corner of the large room, saying, "There's Serna, let's sit by him." We wove around tables until Blake settled his plate across from a dark-haired guy, close to our age, with a broad, gentle smile. "Hey, Grant." Bryce's enthusiasm seemed to have rubbed off on Blake. His voice boomed. "It's great to see you. How's it going?"

"Not bad, Blake." Serna smiled and glanced up. Without standing or reaching over the table for a handshake, he nodded, "You?" I read the casual posture and first name exchange as signs of common ground. "You brought the wife, but where's the kid?"

"At home," Blake said. "We might bring him tomorrow. I just didn't know what this would be like."

"Ridiculous, I'm sure," Serna answered. "If I were you I'd bring the kid just to have an excuse to get outta here."

"Yeah, but leaving him's a pretty good excuse, too, right?" Blake rehearsed his exit strategy, "'Sorry, sir, but we gotta go pick up the kid.'" Serna laughed as Blake glanced at me and added, "That's one of the benefits of having a family. You're done for the night and don't wanna get stupid drunk, you say, 'I gotta get home to the kid.' Anything I want to get out of, I just say, 'gotta get home to the kid.'"

I raised my eyebrows in Serna's direction. "Catches on quick."

"That's Jensen, all right. Catches on quick." Serna lifted his chin in Blake's direction. "So that's why you didn't come up last night? I didn't see you at the bar."

"Yeah, well, we just live in Brookings," Blake explained. "Close enough to drive up this morning. So, how was it? A pretty good time?"

"You know, same old shit. Some guys got pretty wasted. I drank too much." Serna shrugged. "You didn't miss anything. I'm sure you'll catch up tonight."

"Yeah, I don't know. We'll probably go home," Blake said. "I'm not planning to stay for everything. Maybe slip outta here after a while. You know, gotta get the kid."

I wasn't sure why Blake wanted to leave so badly, but there was no time to consider. Our breakfast with Serna was interrupted by an announcement: "Let's all move to the chairs on the west side of the room so we can get started with our first session." We followed orders, depositing our half-eaten breakfast on a side table before settling into a row of chairs in the back, near a wall of windows with the shades pulled down.

After a quick introduction, the lights went out. I'm sure the video that followed, projected on a large screen at the front of the room, began with a man in uniform speaking resolutely about the resources available to soldiers and their families during reintegration. It probably emphasized the importance of the images about to unfold with facts and statistics, which probably would have sounded familiar if I'd read the family readiness pamphlets about PTSD that had come to me in the mail. But as the presentation began to play, it felt like the videos school counselors showed, sometimes, about bus safety or peer pressure, so I was prepared for the overly dramatized, infomercial-ness of it all. A soldier drinking beer in front of the television while a toddler played near a mountain of silver cans. A pre-teen son bounding in the door after school with news about acing a test, his father staring blankly back at him before standing up, retreating to his bedroom, wordlessly shutting the door. Another soldier fighting with his wife over bills and the pressure to provide for his family. A young soldier staggering into an auditorium full of people with a gun tucked into his jacket. What I wasn't prepared for was the reactions I heard. Snickers as a child cried. Giggles as actors yelled and stomped feet. Uproarious laughter as gunshots echoed at the end of a scene.

It was like those first days of kindergarten, when that black cart was wheeled into my classroom, when the thin black box of a VHS was slipped into the VCR, and the images began: a child sneaking along the side of a bus, snowball in hand, planning to launch the white bomb at a friend who pressed his face into glass, but slipping instead down and under, falling out of frame as the bus launched ahead; another, a girl with pigtails, bounding around the corner of the bus with an art project in hand, her blonde curls bouncing as the bus lurched forward, image going blank just before impact. In that sunny kindergarten classroom, I had stared at a nineteen-inch screen, wide-eyed, hearing the jerking fold of bus doors, feeling the trembling bus floor as I timed my step down, smelling the exhaust that met me as my feet hit the ground. My classmates had giggled, much like the soldiers in that convention center did. And after that kindergarten video, I went home, hid in my room, and cried. I couldn't sleep that night, because the video had opened my eyes to things I hadn't even known to fear before.

In that Army video, I saw recognizable slivers of my life too. Blake with a beer in hand. Blake walking trees with a hunting rifle. Blake in the middle of the night, scratching at a wall. And yet those slivers didn't add up to the exaggerated danger presented on screen. Weeks of normalcy and peaceful sleep had convinced me these were not threatening images. Blake was fine. I didn't feel the need to run home and cry, but I couldn't laugh at the possibilities, either. I felt defensive. My guard went up.

The pep talk that followed didn't help. Another clean-cut soldier assured us that we were doing just fine. That we'd make it, as long as we stuck together. "You don't have to face this alone." "We're in this together." "We're here to help." "The worst thing you can do is keep it to yourself." The problems seemed too extreme, the solutions too simple to be taken seriously, fragile clichés that could never bear any real weight.

I was relieved to hear the announcement of a fifteen-minute break. When Blake stood, I did the same. He cupped my elbow and tugged me along toward the hall and the bathroom, and said, "When I come out, let's get outta here." I nodded. This first session had given me just enough time to decide that, while I was glad to have met some of Blake's Army buddies, to have seen him for just a moment in his Army world, he was right. These things were ridiculous. I was ready to retreat. When he emerged and spun towards the exit, I followed, making a conscious effort to walk confidently, like I knew what I was doing and where I was going, but not like I was running away.

Then, at the entrance to the breezeway that would complete our escape, Blake was greeted by a tall, broad-shouldered man who walked hand in hand with a petite, attractive woman. They looked like an all-American couple—a former football captain and varsity cheerleader. Blake slowed to a stop and reached out his hand. I couldn't shake the feeling that we'd been caught, but Blake seemed comfortable, confident. "Hey, good to see you," he smiled, turning his shoulders towards me while maintaining eye contact with the sandy-haired man. "This is my wife, Amber."

The football captain released the cheerleader's hand to shake mine firmly. "It's nice to meet you, Amber." His steady nod, unwavering eye contact calmed me. He turned back to Blake, asking slowly, with genuine concern, "How are things going, Blake? Enjoying family life?"

"Yes, I am," Blake answered, grinning. "And you?"

"Yes, sir," the man answered. "It's good to be home."

The two men looked each other in the eye and smiled, neither of them speaking for a moment. The silence was powerful, but not painful. They studied each other, nodding, unflinching.

Finally, the man smiled and spoke again. "So, you sneaking out, here, Jensen, or what?"

"Yeah," Blake admitted. "But we'll be back, I'm sure."

"Hey, no worries," the All-American said, dismissing us graciously. "You do what you gotta do. But I'm glad I got the chance to see you."

"Yeah, it's great to see you, too," Blake said. "You take care." He slid his fingers through mine and squeezed—a signal to move— and with that we resumed our escape. Outside, Blake slowed his pace, exhaled, and explained. "That was Schild. Brooks Schild."

I lifted my chin toward Blake, signaling my recognition. Brooks Schild. Brother of Richard Schild, who had died in Iraq. "He seems like a good guy," I said, reliving the immediate memory of his firm handshake, his calming magnetism.

"The best," Blake said. "Really, you could never meet a nicer guy. One of the strongest men I've ever met."

"Were you guys close?" I asked.

"Not really," Blake said. "I mean, we never spent much time together or anything, but he just took care of everybody. He was all about details. He drove his guys crazy over details, but it was all to keep them safe. I have a lot of respect for him." Blake looked straight ahead, walking again in a quick clip, as he went on. "When Richard died, Brooks debriefed us," Blake said. "He didn't have to. He could've let somebody else do it. I mean, his brother had just died. But he held it together, like he always did. Kept taking care of guys, like he always did."

I let Blake's words sink in as the memory of the sad story surfaced. My former boss had known the Schild family and told me about the brothers—how Brooks had served in the Iowa National Guard but had been out of service for years when he decided to reenlist to serve beside his brother, Richard. The brothers had roomed together in Iraq, and Brooks said it was a strange sort of blessing, the fact that they were so close in those final days of his life. Now, having met Brooks myself, having witnessed the connection between him and my husband, I formed my own understanding of what it means to serve, to love, to protect, and of what it must feel like to learn that no matter how honorable your service or deep your love, your ability to protect is limited. I realized that I had learned that lesson, too, in my own way. I remembered the wordless, meditative prayer I had prayed when I learned of Richard and Daniel Chuka's deaths, the prayer for strength to move forward. Having just met one of the men I'd been praying for, it felt reassuring, like a benediction. We were all just doing our best to move on and to live in a way that honored those who died.

As we walked toward the car, I linked my arm with Blake's. He felt almost out of reach, but not distant. He felt tall, sturdy, and confident, like in the shelter of his body, I could weather any storm.

ONE NIGHT THAT WINTER, as Blake and Brock washed dishes after supper, I sat at the table, scanning the pages of the *Brookings Register*. I read out loud from an ad, "Bowling League Registration Now Open," playfully suggesting that we should form a team, expecting Blake to laugh. Instead, he raised his eyebrows. "Bowling's fun. We should do it. And we should ask Brad and Liza to be on our team."

"You mean it?"

"Why not?" Blake asked. He motioned to Brock, "We have a built-in-babysitter, living in our basement."

Brock nodded his approval. "I bet Brad would love a bowling league." That statement was even more shocking. Since I officially became part of the Jensen family, Brad had always been painted as a grumpy old man in a young man's body. When I went Christmas shopping with Brock, Brad, and Mark the year before, they warned me as we walked into Walmart that Brad didn't like taking too much time, that I should prepare my shopping list in my head according to store layout so that I would be in and out before Brad got antsy. Brock had warned that if I got almost to the checkout, then remembered I wanted a bag of oranges, I would have to leave the oranges. But Blake was right, Brad and Liza were willing to give bowling a try, so we signed up for the weekly co-ed league.

The first night, Blake and I arrived early. We scanned the lanes, commenting on matching shirts and wrist braces like the ones worn by professional bowlers on TV. Maybe we were in over our heads. At the sound of ball cracking pins, the satisfying clamor that follows a good roll, nerves set in. I remembered the bowling unit in high school Physical Education class, full of gutter balls and dismal scores. I raised my eyebrows at Blake, who stood, hands on hips, nodding slightly. His sharp exhale and bobbing head betrayed a slight sense of intimidation. "OK," he inhaled. "We better find our lane." He clapped his hands.

I nodded in agreement, unsure of exactly how we would do that. "We need shoes, too." I suggested, "I guess we start up at the counter?"

We made our way past racks of balls, most of them well-worn black, some shiny marbled sapphire or magenta. "Yep, you can check in over here on this sheet," the man with a mullet cut at the counter explained as he disinfected bowling shoes, one spritz each. "That will tell you which lane you're on and who you're bowling against this week."

The team listed alongside us had calculated handicaps. I wasn't even sure I remembered how the game was scored.

Blake and I deposited our rental shoes at our lane, then returned to the racks of balls. I settled for a dull, ten pound black one with deep scratches but also a trio of holes that fit what Jerry Seinfeld might have called my man hands. Blake settled on a flashy, swirled blue ball. "Suits you," I teased.

Back at our lane, we whispered to each other as we slipped on brown and red, color-blocked shoes. "So, are we supposed to practice now?"

"I hope so, because it's been years since I've thrown a bowling ball."

"Is that what you call it? Throwing? Or rolling? Do you roll a bowling ball?"

The act of disguising our ignorance brought us closer together, invited us to lean in, brush cheeks, and laugh intimately. "Maybe we should get wrist braces," I suggested, "so we can rip open the Velcro, then reposition everything, strap it back up, like we know what we're doing."

Blake laughed. "Always blame the equipment, Amber. Roll a gutter ball, look all disgusted, adjust the brace."

I buckled toward him, laughing. "Professionals throw gutter balls, too, right?

"And I'm pretty sure any score over ninety is good," he affirmed. We fumbled through warm-ups until Brad and Liza showed up. "Thank God," Blake said. "A couple more misfits."

Brad pretended to be offended. "I don't know what you're talking about. I'm a great bowler." His tenor encouraged Blake, and soon they were both whizzing balls down the lane, comparing their approach steps, their velocity, and their ball spin. Liza and I were just happy to be out of the house, away from studying—me taking a break from rhetorical analysis, Liza from the names and effects of pharmaceuticals. She designated Brad her driver and ordered a mixed drink, which surprised me. The brothers and I shared a pitched of beer. We celebrated successful frames with high fives, failures with wincing inhales and encouraging words. Brad was gracious, and though he was the only one of us to break one hundred, he complimented our progress from frame to frame.

On the way home, Blake said, "That was really fun. Thanks for lining that up."

"It *was* fun," I agreed. "I hadn't really thought about how nice it would be to just hang out with Brad and Liza, actually get to know them." I didn't tell him how much I'd been looking forward to having friends who were a couple, but I was glad for a bowling season's worth of double dates.

Week two of league, Blake and I showed up with our own bowling shoes. I'd bought them online. "Fan-cy," Brad commented.

Liza teased, "Now all you need are argyle socks or something nerdy like that."

"Or shirts," I offered. "Maybe we need matching shirts."

"You could get Cenex to sponsor us, couldn't you Brad?" Blake suggested.

"I don't know," Brad said as he checked the heft of his chosen bowling ball. "I think we might have to bring our averages up, maybe win a match before we pursue sponsorship." We agreed on baby steps. Maybe master our understanding of scoring, first, work on raising our averages to triple digits, then think about team uniforms.

In the meantime, we enjoyed the time together. Watching Blake bowl was a little like watching him play baseball. His long arms didn't seem quite as at home with the pull and release of a bowling ball as they did with the wrist action and follow-through of a baseball swing, and the leg he kicked back to counter the momentum of the bowling ball leaving his hand left him hopping to find balance rather than steady and strong, ready to push forward into a first-base sprint, but the sport of it, the comradery, still gave me an excuse to marvel at him and his fluidity, wrap my arm around his waist in celebration, and encourage him with laughter.

At the end of the night, instead of spending hours flirting in a dugout, Blake and I made our way home. We usually found Brock and George in the rocking chair. Blake would lift George, slumped with sleep, from his uncle's lap and settle him in his bed. Then, after we reported our hopeless bowling scores, Brock recapped his night for us. "What did you feed that kid?" he asked, each night's explosive diaper worse than the week before. "It's unbelievable, the timing. I swear, five minutes after you pull out of the driveway, he loads a diaper for me."

Then, Brock would make his way back downstairs to his bedroom, where a small folding table served as his desk, and study. I studied, too, situating books on the coffee table next to the recliner, computer on my lap, and Blake settled in on the couch to watch TV. In spite of questions and uncertainty—Blake's part-time work and uncertain career path, two years of graduate studies ahead for me—the first months of living together and settling in to married life were reassuring. Promising.

Six

WINTER IN SOUTH DAKOTA CAN BE BEAUTIFUL—frozen landscapes and open skies a canvas to be painted gold and magenta at sunrise—but they can also be brutal—wind cutting temperatures and cracking skin. In late January, as we drove over snow-packed roads from our home in Brookings to Bryant for a weekend of family gatherings, I glanced at George, sleeping in the back seat, then at Blake. "You know how we talked about trying for another baby? How I thought it might take a while?"

Blake stole a quick glance at me, then turned back to the road, a smile tugging at the corners of his mouth, dimples cutting into his cheeks. "I remember."

"Well, it didn't."

"Seriously?"

"Seriously," I said. I still couldn't believe it. When I took the pregnancy test earlier that day, Blake was still at work. I didn't think he needed to be there. I wasn't expecting a positive result.

Blake squinted, his head bobbing slightly from side to side as he counted. "So that means, what, November?"

"Pretty good on the fast math," I teased. Blake's quick calculation had been a long-standing joke since he was in Iraq, when I explained to him that the packages I sent usually took a week to get to him and that I'd sent one the day before, a Wednesday. He'd actually counted out loud—I pictured his fingers dipping, one at a time—then he said, "So it should get here next Wednesday?" "Yes, Blake," I'd laughed. "Seven days equals one week, and next Wednesday is one week from this Wednesday." I smiled at the memory as I corrected his calculation. "Nine months from now would be October. That seems to be a good month for us." George had been born in October.

"It's a good month," Blake agreed.

"But it's gonna be crazy," I said. "You know, I'll still have my thesis to write. I don't know how I'll do it." Blake assured me we'd make it work. "But let's not tell anyone," I said. "I need to get used to the idea."

The truth was, I wasn't sure how I felt. Over the coming weeks as I sat in our living room, my legs going numb under the weight of textbooks, my eyelids falling shut and my comments on Freshman Comp essays trailing off into blue streaks of ink when I dozed off in the middle of grading, I worried. Maternity leave wasn't a question when George was born. I'd had a full-time job, but leave wasn't built into a graduate school plan. Excitement countered concern when I pictured a baby girl with my dark eyes and blonde hair, Blake's wide grin. What would we name her? If it was a boy, I knew Blake would lobby for Louis, after his paternal great-grandfather, but we'd never seriously discussed names for a girl. I imagined Blake, a newborn cradled in his arms, and I smiled, thinking, at least we'll be together this time.

Morning sickness was mild, which seemed to relieve Blake but worried me. When I woke to a wrenching stomach one morning in March, I was almost relieved. But the pain felt less like nausea, more like cramps. As Blake dressed for work, I curled up at the end of the bed, clenching my gut. "I thought I was getting by easy this time, but I feel awful. Maybe you should be miserable with me. Wanna call in sick?"

Blake smiled as he zipped his coat. "I better not," he said, patting my foot as I curled back under the covers. "You'll be OK, right?"

I relented. "Yeah, I'll be fine."

Blake switched the light off as he left the room, and I listened to the squeal of the back door, the turn of the engine and tires crunching the fresh snow that had fallen during the night. When I couldn't get back to sleep, I decided to work through the pain. George was still sleeping, and the sidewalk needed shoveling. Halfway through the dense, wet snow, the ache in my back tightened into a cramp, so I excused myself from the work, reasoning that George could wake up at any time. I shuffled toward the house, and as I reached for the doorknob, I realized it wasn't the weight of the snow, it wasn't concern for George that brought me inside. My abdomen curled in on itself, pulling me down to a crouch. I staggered to the bathroom, boots squealing over ceramic tile, and felt the spot of blood seep from me before I made it there. When I did, I confirmed the feeling. I was bleeding.

I told myself not to panic. I'd read that spotting was normal in early pregnancy, something about one pad with slight spotting over several hours being no cause for alarm. But as George woke up and we began our morning ritual of reading and rocking in the living room recliner, normalcy vanished. A spot developed into clots of deep red. By the time my doctor returned my call, I'd had to change my blood-stained sweatpants. I knew what was happening.

I lined the recliner, already spotted with blood, with a towel, covered myself with the quilt my grandmother had stitched for my high school graduation, and called Blake. "Can you come home? Something's wrong. I called my sister, she's taking me to the doctor."

His response was simple. "I'll be there soon." He didn't ask any questions or make me say, Blake, I'm losing the baby. He just came. I imagined his eyes following the painted white border of the interstate over hills, around curves, and beyond the horizon, squinting toward a place in the future where everything will be all right, seeing that place like he always did, even when I didn't believe it existed.

We spent the afternoon in exam and waiting rooms, listening to doctors and nurses who tried to give us hope, but by the time the ultrasound tech confirmed with her words—*we can't detect a heartbeat*—I'd already begun to move from mourning to acceptance. *Maybe this is best*, I told myself. *Maybe something was wrong with the baby. Maybe this is why everything felt so strange.*

Laying against a stiff mattress, abdomen exposed, I imagined George sleeping on Blake's shoulder in the waiting room outside, his body ironing wrinkles into his dad's button-up plaid. I summoned the soft static of Blake's fingertips circling the surface of my skin to replace the hospital sheets scratching my lower back, the hot weight of George's sleeping body to protect me from the cold air that poured from a vent overhead. I tried to imagine away the machines and measurement, but the slather of thick gel, the shocking cold of plastic, the smell of sterilization grounded me there. The voice of the ultrasound technician, barely audible above the hum and click of technology, commanded my attention. "The fetus stopped growing at about five weeks."

I turned toward the glow of the monitor, remembering my first ultrasound, the pixilated image of George's fingers flexing across the screen. This time I saw no miracle there. Only fuzzy, grey flecks spitting shadows.

When we returned to the duplex, I was afraid to speak, afraid to ask the questions rattling in my brain—*Is it better this way? Were we ready? Was something wrong?*—afraid to acknowledge my combined sadness and acceptance. So, I perched in a nest of blankets and pillows, pressed a heating pad into my stomach, and rocked. Blake sat on the couch, flipping between adult cartoons, the Food Network, and the History Channel. I stared past him at the white stripes of our vertical blinds, let my eyes lose focus. He kept the volume low, asked if I needed anything, and when I shook my head from side to side and closed my eyes, he accepted my answer quietly.

I recognized the silence. It was the silence of unnamable understanding, the silence that two people who've been through hell together can sit comfortably in. No judgment, no blame. No shame. I hadn't stopped to consider what Blake felt he'd lost, whether or not he felt connected to the baby, or if he'd been picking names. But whatever he was feeling, I knew he understood. That's why he didn't try to fix it. He knew it was unfixable. He made himself available to me but didn't insist that I need him. He stayed close, willing to break the silence, take action, or willing to stay still, look me in the eye, and inhabit silence with me. Silence felt like love.

When Blake's phone rang, he stepped into the kitchen to answer. His side of the conversation comforted me: "No, she's all right. Or she will be. You know, this happens sometimes. We'll figure it out. And really, we'll be fine." I listened as Blake thanked his boss for calling, then flipped his phone shut and slid it onto the kitchen counter before he returned to the living room.

When he slipped onto the couch, I opened my eyes. I wanted to say, *Thank you*, but instead I offered him a smile. He flipped through channels, settling on *House Hunters*. "Which house do you think they'll go with?" he asked, as the smooth-voiced host reviewed the couple's choices.

"The second one," I said. "It's got everything they need. Just needs a little remodeling."

As we sat in the empty space created by the miscarriage, together, never talking directly about it, I thought about Blake's experiences in Iraq. I'd often doubted myself, wondering if I should know more, if I should ask, feeling I was doing something wrong, missing something. But as I experienced the comfort of quiet understanding, I decided to let go of that doubt, to trust silence and the space it creates for healing.

As a Midwesterner, a descendant of Scandinavians, and a South Dakota farm girl, it was easy to do. For me, noise was the bellow of a calf piercing nighttime quiet or cottonwood leaves whispering in a breeze. In my family, conversation was peppered with long pauses. While teaching English in Mexico, I'd learned through a Cambridge teacher training that Scandinavian language learners scored lower on oral exams when reviewers weren't familiar with their cultural acceptance of silence. Silence could be misinterpreted as an inability to communicate, a lack of understanding, but sometimes it was a sign of listening and contemplation. That insight had transformed my own understanding. My cousin Brad had always joked that when my dad introduced himself on the phone, the person on the other end might think he'd fallen asleep midsentence because of the long pause between the initial "Hi, this is Win" and the clarification, "Win Noem." Blake had enjoyed his months working with my dad and their long, quiet drives for deliveries. Silence wasn't always a bad thing. Sometimes silence created connection.

Maybe the truly surprising thing was how long it took me to appreciate silence, to stop questioning it. Or maybe part of me understood silence as a double-edged sword, sensed its potentially dangerous edges. The calm before a storm. The cacophony that shatters silence held too long.

FOR ME, AS A PARENT, the silence of nighttime could be terrifying. Sometimes I would wake at night and listen for the rustle of sheets to assure me that George was sleeping but alive. The idea of SIDS terrified me. If George was too quiet at night, sometimes I made my way to his doorway, or crept to the side of his bed where I could study his body, watch his chest raise and lower to assure me he was breathing. In the morning, the slightest sound from his room would yank me from sleep, pull me to his bedside so that he might wake up feeling secure, and not fearful and alone.

What I didn't hear those mornings, or what didn't register as sound, was the shuffle of Blake's feet. When Blake woke up, he slid his legs off the bed and stood slowly, his back locked straight, and shuffled around the house, like the old men in the nursing home where I worked in high school, men whose slippered feet slid over the surface of the floor, inching their way toward the dining room. Blake was twenty-eight years old, and he was walking like an old man. When the sound did begin to register, I only noticed it in the morning. But by spring, when Blake began spending longer hours working with his dad and brother on the farm, working for my dad in his agronomy office, and playing baseball with the amateur team he'd played with since high school, the shuffling became the norm at night too. Blake lifted himself from the couch and asked, "Are you ready for bed?" and as I switched off the TV and made my way down the hall, Blake would follow slowly, his feet dragging over hardwood floors that squeaked under the weight of his body. From the bedroom, I could hear the scrub of bristles over teeth, the swish and spit of fluoride, followed by the rattle of pill bottles.

I didn't think much of the pill bottles at first, either. After his discharge physical, Blake was diagnosed with degenerative disk disease, rated with ten percent disability, and sent home with a prescription for pain medication, orders for physical therapy. I had experienced back pain all my life with surgery at the age of thirteen, so back pain wasn't foreign to me. I'd learned to live with mine, and I assumed initially that Blake would do the same. But one day I went to the medicine cabinet for ibuprofen to ease a headache and found the bottle I'd recently purchased almost empty.

"Did your prescriptions from the VA run out, or what?" I asked Blake.

"No, I've still got them, still take them, but they don't help much," he explained nonchalantly. "They take the edge off, but they don't really stop the pain."

"So, you take ibuprofen, too?" I asked and shook the empty pill bottle. Blake nodded. "How much?"

"Not that much."

"How much?" I insisted.

"Depends. Six, maybe, but not usually during the day. Just at night, so I can sleep."

I could tell this seemed normal to him.

"If I have a game, if I think I'll actually have to play, I take some then, too, a couple hours before the game so I can loosen up. I'm not sure it helps."

"You're serious? Six? At a time? That can't be good for you. You can't do that all your life, Blake. It'll kill your stomach." I cringed at the reprimanding tone of my voice.

"It's not that bad," he scoffed. "Just ibuprofen, it's not gonna kill me."

"Yeah, but if it's that bad, you have to go back to the doctor. They have to give you something better, something that helps more."

"You're right," Blake answered. "You're absolutely right." This was another sound I got used to hearing: Blake agreeing only to pacify me. I didn't understand his reluctance.

When Blake came home from Iraq, I hadn't given much thought to the term disability. He'd come home alive. No bullet wounds, no shrapnel. He'd never even dropped a helmet on his toe. With no visible injuries, he seemed fine. He seemed normal. Despite the scare on his first night home, Blake showed no on-going signs of PTSD. As weeks gave way to months, months to years, Blake seemed perfectly well adjusted. But as his back pain became more obvious, I began to think about disability differently—as something invisible, almost undetectable, but life altering. The physical changes came slowly, almost imperceptibly. First, he stopped golfing, making the excuse that he was a husband and a father, no time for eighteen holes of golf each week. He played fewer innings of baseball, stretching for half an hour before each game, and afterwards, lying flat on the ground as if he couldn't imagine getting up. But the changes seemed inevitable, a natural part of aging, even, and he still enjoyed being around the sport, sharing his love of the game with his son, who seemed, naturally, to love it too.

The first time George saw a real dugout, he wanted to follow his dad down. The Bucs were playing in Aurora, the last amateur park I knew of in the state with real dugouts, sunken into the ground. I'd led George to the metal bleachers along the third base line while Blake descended the cement stairs with his baseball bag, but as his father was swallowed by shadows, George twisted his body and kicked his legs until he wiggled his way to the grass, clawing after Blake. It was almost as if George understood the rarity, the treasure of memories, as if he wanted to feel what his dad and his uncle Brock had felt when they were kids and their dad played amateur ball. Then, Bryant still had real dugouts, too, and Brock and Blake stood at the top of those cement stairs, handing bats and helmets to their dad and his teammates as they emerged.

Between innings they descended to fill their cheeks with sunflower seeds and Big League Chew. Sometimes they sat on the slightly pitched roof, just a foot above ground, other times they descended, listening to the crunch of cleats, splash of saliva, and the crack of the bat from the same vantage point as their dad; observing from that special place that separated players from fans, that place that must have tickled their nostrils with the combined scents of dust, cigarette smoke, and sweat. In that dugout, they were educated in the swallowed sound of baseball banter, the way lips pinched back words like hey-whaddya-say-now so they rumbled at the back of the throat. Suddenly, upon seeing a real dugout, George wanted to experience it all too.

I'd heard stories from Brock and Blake about being batboys for their dad's baseball team. I'd heard Brock imagine how great it must be for Blake to share that with his own son. "That's gotta be an awesome feeling," Brock said, "when your own kids look up to you like that."

And I saw it in action, as George started to follow the game enough to cheer for his dad. He sat behind home plate, yelling, "Hit a homerun Daddy! Hit a homerun!" over and over again until Blake's at bat ended.

Brock talked about it after games, saying, "I remember that. Sitting there, thinking, That's my dad."

"Yeah, but it's kind of a lot of pressure," Blake joked. "That's why I've gotta end my baseball career, right now, while George still assumes his dad hits homeruns, before he figures out how to say, 'Dad struck out.'" Laughter masked the truth. When Blake emerged from the dugout, looking tall and lean in pinstriped pants and a Kelly green Bucs jersey, George scrambled over to him, glove in hand, but Blake didn't say, "Wanna play some catch, kid?" He asked me for ibuprofen.

LOADED SILENCE CONTINUED TO BUILD. One afternoon of the following summer, after lunch at my father-in-law's house, I watched George step carefully down the cement steps, his hand dragging along the wobbly silver railing, knowing better than to depend on it for support. He'd walked those stairs enough times to know that the rail could give out at any moment.

George was on his way outside to warm up for the game of Wiffle ball that he'd been promised would begin as soon as his dad, Uncle Brock, and I cleaned up the kitchen. I paused at the window to watch George, who jogged across the yard, his wiry arms dangling at his sides, not drawn up and pumping back and forth in usual running fashion. "It's official. George has inherited his dad's signature run," I said, recognizing the singular, straight-armed trot that made Blake easy to identify as he ran across the outfield.

Brock laughed and peered over my shoulder, "Yep, stiff-armed but lightning fast, just like his dad."

"And look how cute," I said, motioning toward the window at George, balanced in a lunging position. "He's stretching."

Brock turned again to check George's pre-game routine. "He's serious about this, Amber. Nobody wants a pulled muscle."

I returned to the sink, immersing my hands in the dish soap that bubbled from a frying pan, when Brock burst into a laugh. "Oh, that's hilarious," he said between peals of laughter. "Blake, you've gotta see this." Blake and I stepped to the window to find George, hands on hips, leaning his torso back and to each side. He repeated the motion several times, slowly, then hunched his shoulders forward and squinted, wincing with imaginary pain. Brock glanced at Blake. "What does that tell you?"

"That George needs a backiotomy too?" Blake joked, employing his brother's term for the imaginary back replacement surgery that the VA would offer to alleviate Blake's pain.

"Poor kid thinks that's normal," Brock said. "His dad's a cripple, so he thinks he should be too."

We laughed it off.

When Blake was issued a battery-operated nerve stimulator to loosen his muscles and lessen his pain, we laughed at that too. When he adjusted electrode patches along his spine or fiddled with the small, black control box in his pocket, turning electrical currents on and off at fifteen-minute intervals as per doctor's orders, we teased. "Behold, the bionic man."

"You should try it," he told me. "You like massages and stuff, maybe you'd like this."

"Does it help?" I asked.

"It might. You'd probably like it."

"No, I mean, does it help you? Does it feel good?"

"It doesn't feel bad," he said. "I'm not sure it really helps, but it's not bad."

After a few weeks, a month maybe, he grew tired of being bionic. The VA suggested steroid injections. He tried them. Again, no results. He continued pain medication, supplemented with ibuprofen. Still no relief.

That summer, Blake slid into a managerial role on the Bucs baseball team, only taking the field when they were short players. He claimed strategy. It was hard to keep an amateur team going in a small town, so the young guys needed playing time. If they didn't improve themselves, didn't enjoy coming to games, the team would dwindle out. I was less concerned about the future of Bucs baseball than I was about my husband letting go of something he loved so much.

"You need to be honest about how bad it is," I urged before each VA appointment. "They'll never know unless you tell them. I mean people with stupid injuries—like broken toes or things that don't even bother them—get more disability than you do."

I wasn't the only one who noticed. Brock told me Blake needed to get his disability rating reevaluated. My uncle, who had served in Vietnam, warned that Blake needed to get things documented sooner rather than later to ensure that the increasing severity was recorded as a service-related injury. I pleaded with Blake, "You need to advocate for yourself. There has to be something they can do."

The more I pushed, the more Blake resisted. The conversation became a regular one, and even though I hated telling Blake what to do, I kept insisting, until one night he presented his side of the argument. "You're right, Amber. I should get it reevaluated," he said. "But I'm not gonna be that guy. I mean, I know guys who get ridiculous amounts of disability, guys who are supposedly messed up, PTSD or whatever, and their lives really aren't that bad. They're just playing the system."

My insistence was interrupted momentarily while I defended the position of these nameless soldiers. "That's not fair. You don't know for sure. You don't know what their lives are like. Maybe it *is* that bad, they just keep it together on the outside." I raised my eyebrows to remind Blake of his own masquerade.

"No, I'm talking about guys who've never seen anything, never even been in a real war zone," he explained. "One hundred percent disability. It's just stupid."

"OK," I conceded. "I hear what you're saying. But combat isn't the only form of trauma, and PTSD isn't the only kind of disability. Sometimes disabilities aren't visible from the outside."

"Yeah, that's fine," Blake said. "But I'm not gonna be that guy."

We were approaching the same subject from different angles. Blake was dutiful, his service honorable. I wanted him to recognize that those things made him deserving—of compensation? Maybe. Of a comfortable life? Definitely. He didn't see those things as unique. He didn't see himself as deserving of any reward or requiring any sympathy. And in a way, he was right. In comparison to some soldiers, Blake was fine. We were fine. He was able to work. We were getting by financially. He didn't want to talk about disability, or dwell on something he could work through. He wanted to move on, play whatever innings he could play, and live. And so, we did.

I followed Blake's lead. He had one rule for coaching George in baseball: "Don't ever correct him on his swing, Amber. Make sure he's facing the right way, get his hands in the right place on the bat, but other than that, just let him swing. The worst thing you can do is get a kid thinking too much about it. He's just gotta swing until he figures it out."

I relented, sensing that I had no choice but to let Blake swing the bat, and hoped to hear the crack of solid contact.

WHEN FALL CAME, I sat one night, buried beneath a Shakespeare anthology and piles of articles printed from the library database. When Blake turned off the TV, I assumed he was going to bed. Instead, he said, "I have to ask you for a favor." He spoke low and quiet, like it was hard to get the words out. I lifted my chin in his direction and raised my eyebrows, signaling that I was listening but reluctant. My fingers hovered over laptop keys, pausing in my struggle to analyze the sacred oaths made in *Arden of Faversham*.

"OK," I said, preparing myself to deflect a request to iron his dress shirt for work the next day.

When Blake explained, "I need you to help me write a letter," I rolled my eyes. Blake and I labored for hours over the logic and grammar in the letters his boss, his Uncle Les, drafted. Les was a retired military man with an impressive career—thirty years of service in the South Dakota Army National Guard, appointment as South Dakota's adjutant general, and inspiration for Blake's own military service—and he wrote the same way he spoke: like a motivational speaker. When Blake brought a letter home, it meant it needed balance between the formality of business correspondence and Les's strong voice. That night, facing a deadline of my own, I didn't feel up to the challenge.

"Can it wait until tomorrow?" I asked. I knew I should play my role as supportive wife. I loved that Blake appreciated my writing skills. It reminded me of the first time I asked him to edit one of my papers for graduate school, how he shook his head, making me nervous that the argument was unconvincing, supporting evidence flimsy, before surprising me by saying, "Amber, they're killing you. The paper is fine. Your argument is good. But this doesn't sound like you, like the letters you sent me. I read those over and over again, but this is killing you." I usually enjoyed sitting next to Blake on the couch, connecting emotionally and intellectually over revisions, but that night, I didn't have time. "I've got to finish this paper for class tomorrow."

"I know. But I'd like to get it over with," Blake said, his voice quiet. "I need to write a letter to my commander." He paused, maybe hoping that in spite of my well-established military ignorance he wouldn't have to explain. I stared, wide-eyed, completely confused. Blake clarified. "I need to write a letter asking for release. To get out of the Army."

Resentment shifted to relief. My first thought was no more deployment. But I was also shocked. I'd been devastated when Blake, still in Iraq at the time, told me over the phone that he was extending his military service. He'd lead with the words, "So, I need to talk to you about something. I mean, I've made up my mind, but I feel like I should talk to you about it first." His voice was so apologetic that I thought he was going to say he wanted a divorce, so I was relieved when he said, "I'm gonna re-up. Enlist for six more years." The news had shattered me, and yet, when he explained his reasoning—that this way, even though he didn't have a steady job arranged for when he got home, he could feel like he was providing for George and I, health insurance, at least, plus a small monthly income—as much as I'd hated it, I knew he was right. He was still there, in a war zone, and if he was willing to re-sign in the midst of that, he must have been sure. There was nothing to do but be proud of his commitment. And now, three years later, he was getting out. I was confused.

Blake had talked about getting out of the Army, most often when he was frustrated by a shit show of a guard drill—too much hurry up and wait—or questioning higher ups who seemed disorganized. He and Brock complained about leadership in the new unit they'd been transferred to. Brock said there was no way he'd ever go overseas with that bunch of clowns, and he didn't want Blake to, either. "He either needs to transfer, apply for a full time Army job, or just get out," Brock had warned. "This unit's gonna get deployed eventually, and it's a disaster waiting to happen."

But neither of them had made any move. Until now, when Blake stared at the floor and said, "I'd really like to just get it over with tonight, put the letter in the mail tomorrow."

I set my Shakespeare anthology aside. "Of course," I said. "Where do we start?"

I thought the letter itself would be simple. Dear so-and-so, I am writing to submit my request for release from the South Dakota Army National Guard. But what I approached as a simple resignation letter required, in Blake's eyes, full rhetorical analysis: impeccable word choice, emotional appeals, air-tight logic. I hadn't realized that the letter required persuasion.

"They don't have to let me out," Blake said. "They'd be stupid not to, but they don't have to."

So, we carefully constructed the argument. I tried to put family and career at the forefront; Blake resisted. He wanted to clarify that his employer was not denying him advancement in his career because of his commitment to the military, because that really wasn't the case, but that he, personally, felt unable to commit fully to his new career while in the military. He added, as a side note, that since his back injury would disqualify him for deployment, prolonging his commitment to the National Guard seemed futile.

"Is that true?" I asked.

"Oh, yeah. I'd never pass a pre-deployment physical." He explained, "There's no way I could wear the Kevlar. They'd be stupid to send me. And they never would. So why waste my weekends when I'm no good to the Army anyway?"

"But is your back really that bad?" I was studying him now. This wasn't a new conversation, but new context.

"Absolutely," he said. "There's no way I'm deployable."

I pushed, "But if it's that bad, then why isn't someone helping you? Shouldn't the VA be doing more?"

Blake looked away. I understood. We returned to the task at hand.

Organization, precision, concision. I proposed language, Blake accepted or rejected. And as he polished and revised, I realized this letter wasn't just paperwork to be filed with human resources—not a letter of resignation but an *act* of resignation. I remembered watching Blake and Brock shoot fireworks with George on the Fourth of July, how they lit Army tanks and reminisced about the narratives they would shape as kids, lighting those same cardboard tanks, watching them fire their sparkly cannons, then burst into flames. "Oh no, he's not gonna make it. Get outta there!" The bottle rocket wars they fought with other Bryant boys, storing up ammunition of whistlers and roman candles. The uncle whose war stories they repeated. The movies they watched. The books they read. They'd been playing Army their whole lives. This resignation was a reshaping of identity. Blake was justifying his decision as much to himself as to anyone else.

Once the letter was printed, signed, and sealed in an envelope, Blake said, "Thank you. I couldn't have done that alone."

I smiled tentatively. I was happy to help, but new language, new concern, nagged at me. Non-deployable. A non-threatening threat. A bomb that would not detonate.

Seven

EVEN THE MOST EMINENT STORMS DISSIPATE, sometimes. Electricity builds and pressure releases. Rain cools the atmosphere, sometimes in a raging storm, other times in the form of gentle showers, but the potential for destruction and nourishment both implied in the same sky. For Blake and I, potential came in pregnancy. We were expecting our second child—a girl this time. Potential also came professionally. Blake took on new responsibilities, managing retirement plans and conducting client meetings, and I accepted a new part-time teaching job, which I would balance with online classes as I worked toward a master of fine arts in creative writing. All of this created opportunity and obligation that pulled us forward.

On October 6, we sat in a small pink room, preparing to welcome our daughter into the world. After six chaotic weeks of family commuting from Brookings to Sioux Falls—fifty-five miles each way—and after negotiating the purchase of our first home, which we would close on the week after our daughter was born—the hospital created a cocoon of excited calm. Within hours, we would be a family of four. Four weeks of maternity leave would give us time to settle into new routines and a new house. Life paused as we prepared for change.

While we waited for the doctor, I teased Blake. "There's no getting out of this now. The delivery room's just a few minutes away."

He shrugged. "I still say its surgery. I'm not a doctor, I probably shouldn't be in there."

"You're pathetic," I laughed. "But go ahead and run your theory by Dr. Wierda if you want."

Blake nodded through his explanation. "All I know is my dad had four kids and never went in the delivery room. I bet your dad never did, either. Nothing wrong with tradition."

I raised my eyebrows. "Nothing wrong with change, either. You'll be glad once you're there. And," I paused for emphasis, "you'll take pictures. You're not getting out of that, either." Blake looked skeptical.

"It will be fine. At least it's a C-section," I reminded him. Blake had been relieved when our doctor suggested the procedure, which he thought alleviated him of responsibility. No coaching me through breathing and pushing.

With a quick knock, Dr. Wierda entered, flipping through my chart. "Are we ready to have a baby today?"

I smiled and nodded. Blake patted his knees nervously at the edge of the bed. Dr. Wierda smiled and reassured, "Everything looks good. Let's just listen to the heartbeat." Sliding the stethoscope over my belly, she looked surprised. "This one's an acrobat. She's flipped—head down, now." She inhaled, "That must have been uncomfortable."

I shook my head, "I didn't notice anything. Are you sure?"

Of course, she was sure. She smiled, "Yes, and, just so you know, that could change things, give you some options. We could go ahead with the C-section, or we could induce labor, or you could go home and wait. Do you want to try for a vaginal birth?"

I knew the anatomical description alone would make Blake uncomfortable. I didn't have to turn to him to know what his answer would be. But my gut said *no* too. I was anxious to hold my daughter in my arms. I'd even decided on her name, finally. I couldn't just go home and wait.

Dr. Wierda read our expressions and nodded. "You don't want to wait. I understand." She added, "With a previous C-section, there's no telling what would happen. We could end up doing one anyway. We'll just go ahead with our original plan." She looked at me, then Blake, who nodded emphatically. "The anesthesiologist will be in soon to bring you down."

When the doctor left, I turned to Blake, laughing. "Your daughter's messing with you even before she's born?"

"Yeah," he said. "She's trying to change the game on us, but we have to hold firm, make sure she knows who's boss."

I couldn't help but laugh at my husband, who feigned toughness while squirming in a boxy, mauve chair. Since he was already uncomfortable, I threw out a question I knew he'd rather avoid. "Can you believe you missed out on this when George was born? Do you ever think about that?"

"Not really," Blake shook his head. I doubted his confidence, reading it as misplaced or, at best, unexamined. I wondered if holding our newborn daughter, watching her eyes learn to focus, her fingers learn to grasp, hearing her first coos and gurgles would make him realize what he'd missed with his son. I couldn't help but fear imbalance—Blake bonding more with our daughter than he had with George—but I hoped for renewed appreciation too, the miracle of birth and infancy filling some void in Blake's understanding of parenthood.

As if sensing the spiral of my thoughts, Blake defended his position. "I saw George kick plenty of times. I saw the pictures. He was all slimy at first, he went through his ugly phase, like dogs do, but he had that perfectly round head." Another serious topic deflected with jokes. "George never drooled on me or pooped on me. Easiest baby in the history of the world." For four years, he'd made light of missing George's birth, and in many ways, Blake was right, he didn't seem to have missed out. He and George enjoyed each other's company. They were fine. We were fine. So, we moved on.

When the anesthesiologist entered, handing Blake his blue smock and pants, a mask, hat, and shoe covers, he explained, "While they're getting Amber ready, you can slip these on, then someone will bring you down to the operating room. By that time, the epidural should be in place, and things will happen pretty fast." Blake forced a smile. I squeezed his knee and said, "I'll see you down there." Then as the nurse wheeled me out of the room, I turned to remind him, "Don't forget the camera."

In the operating room, I surveyed the country-blue, eighties décor. I remembered it differently—all stainless steel, modern—but this seemed sort of quaint. Welcoming. What hadn't changed was the nervous feeling that swelled in me when the anesthesiologist instructed me to slide to the edge of the table and hunch my back. I hated the idea of a needle slipping into my spine and wished Blake was there with me. I pictured him, dressing in his hospital blues and thought, *He's here, this time. Just a few minutes, and he'll be in.*

And he was. When Blake appeared at my side, he squeezed my hand and raised his eyebrows, his puffy blue cap lifting, mask inflating as he exhaled audibly. "It's not that bad," I promised.

The nurse assured him, too. "You can stay right here beside your wife. You don't have to look past the curtain if you don't want to." She pointed at the blue barrier hanging above my rib-cage. Then she looked at me and said, "Don't worry—we've got the camera." Blake looked sheepish as she placed it in his hands. "You're not the first nervous dad we've had."

I shook my head at Blake, but before I could say anything,

the routine of checking the feeling in my legs was underway. The anesthesiologist at my feet said, "Let's see how were doing, I'm just going to pinch your heel. Let me know if you feel anything."

As a nurse strapped my arms to the operating table, I concentrated on the legs I couldn't move. "Yeah, I felt that." Blake crouched closer to me. "I hate this part," I whispered. "I swear I felt that, but they're going to say I didn't." His mask fluttered as he sucked in air. His uncertainty was endearing.

When the doctor said, "I think we're ready to go." I closed my eyes. Blake huddled close to my temple, our collectively held breath as close to Lamaze as we'd ever get.

Then, suddenly, Dr. Wierda exclaimed, "Look at all that hair!" and held our chubby, blue-tinged girl momentarily over the curtain. Blake raised his eyebrows, as if to say, *That's it? That's all it takes?*

I wanted to pull him toward me, but I was strapped down, crucifixion style. "She's here," I grinned, as our daughter wailed. Blake turned toward the sound, and within seconds, a tight, red-faced bundle landed in his arms. His expression was soft, surprised, every bit as enraptured as I dreamed he would be.

The rapture was broken when a nurse instructed Blake to pose next to me. She snapped a picture, then asked "Do we have a name?"

"Addelyn," I said. "Addelyn Ruth."

The nurse affirmed with a nod, then turned to Blake. "OK, Dad. Let's trade." She held out a camera, lifted Addie from Blake's arms. He stood as directed and disappeared in the direction she pointed. She turned to me and smiled. "Proud daddy. We'll take him with us down to the nursery, and then they'll meet you in the recovery room in a few minutes."

AS SOON AS THEY WERE GONE, my typical post-op nausea set

in. After I puked, one nurse tilted the bed to try to alleviate my discomfort, while another stitched up my incision. Soon, I was wheeled to the recovery room where, after just a few moments alone, my mom and sister entered, leading George by the hand. "Hi buddy," I said, patting the mattress next to me. "Did you see baby Addie?"

"Yeah," he answered quietly, leaning toward me. He reached out to touch my hospital bracelets.

"Is it weird to see mommy in a hospital bed?" I asked.

"Yeah," he whispered.

"Don't worry. I'm just tired after having the baby. Did you see your daddy?" Uncertain, he looked at my mom, who nodded.

"We saw him in the nursery with Addie, didn't we?"

"Yeah," George smiled slightly now. "Addie was crying."

"They'll bring her in here in a couple minutes," I told George. "And then you'll get to hold her, and then I bet she won't cry anymore."

I'd forgotten about this reality of C-section birth—the disconnect of not being able to hold this newborn child. Picturing Blake with her was reassuring, but I wanted them both there with me. All of us, together.

As we waited, Erin asked, "So did Blake peek over the curtain during the delivery?"

"Are you kidding?" I laughed. "You never did. Did you honestly think Blake would?"

As if he sensed our conversation and wanted to step in to defend himself, Blake appeared at the foot of the bed. The nurse followed, wheeling a bassinet to the side of my bed. When she lifted Addelyn and placed her in my arms, George followed the movement, as if hypnotized. He climbed onto the mattress, clamoring to see his baby sister.

My sister and mom stepped to the edge of the curtained room and snapped pictures as Blake, George, and I huddled around Addie, admiring her pursed lips and alert eyes, the way she flexed her fingers and clenched them into tight fists. Blake's anxiety disappeared, the concern melted from George's face, and I stopped comparing. For the moment, at least.

TWO WEEKS LATER, back at our duplex, I woke in the recliner when a bead of sweat skated over my skin, tickling my chest. Details registered: Addie's hot forehead, her fine, dark hair damp with sweat, cheeks clammy. Thinking I'd swaddled her too tightly, I uncoiled fleece, but her neck and arms were hot to the touch. Her hand, even. I lunged to the bathroom and began fumbling through half empty boxes and bottles of medicine, finding three dead thermometers before, finally, one with working batteries. I slipped Addie's arm from her sleeper and tucked the cool plastic into her armpit.

101.2 degrees.

I pulled my laptop from the coffee table and searched infant temperature tables. The first two sites warned that any temp over one hundred degrees was serious for an infant of her age. They both said, "Contact your doctor immediately."

Immediately.

Still, I reasoned, Addie had been nursing well all night, wide-eyed as usual after each feeding, studying my face and the bright slivers of light beaming in from the street. She had to be fine. Surely the fever would come down with Tylenol, the doctor's visit could wait for acute care in the morning.

I felt Addie's flushed skin and checked her temperature again: 101.4. Holding her high on my chest, my cheek tucked against her forehead, I carried her to the kitchen and fished a phonebook from the junk drawer. Thin pages rattled as I searched for Ask-A-Nurse. I dialed the number, just in case. I reported the fever and Addie's normal sleeping, eating, and alertness, but when a nurse returned my call, she lowered her voice and spoke slowly. "That fever is dangerously high for a baby at two weeks. You must take her in." Her tone was urgent. "This shouldn't wait until morning."

My heart swelled, each of its beats hammering the walls of my chest, sending tingles through me, and making my ears ring. I grabbed the diaper bag and buckled Addie in her car seat. Her tiny body radiated heat, but I slid a fleece hat over her damp hair and tucked a flannel quilt around her shoulders and up under her feet. I wiggled my bare feet into tennis shoes, zipped my coat, and started out the door before I paused and remembered Blake.

I placed Addie's seat near the back door, then crept towards our bedroom. With weight balanced on the balls of my feet, careful not to creak the floorboards, I felt my way to Blake's side of the bed and hovered over him, whispering, "Addie's sick. I'm taking her to the emergency room."

His answer was sluggish, almost inaudible. "OK," he said.

"I think she's fine, but I'll call you when I know more."

"What's wrong?"

"She has a fever," I said. Blake squinted through the dark like he didn't recognize me, as if I resembled someone he used to know, but he couldn't quite place me. I stood and said, "I guess you should stay here with George."

Although I was the one who'd almost left the house without telling him, I wished he would offer to come, even if he didn't get out of bed. Instead, he answered, "Well, call if you need anything," his voice slowed with sleep. He flipped onto his side, tucking one corner of the quilt over his own head, the other around George, who had snuck from his bed into ours. George wiggled backwards until he was curled into his dad's chest. I leaned over to kiss my son's cheek, then drifted back through the dark, and lifted Addie's car seat and rushing out the door.

At the emergency room, technicians tested Addie's blood and attempted a urine sample, then explained that a spinal tap might be necessary. "If it's an infection, we need to find out the source right away. Infection could mean a lot of things." Spinal tap sounded serious. The ER doctor seemed disgusted with me, as if I'd done something wrong. Or maybe just serious, preparing me for the worst. Or maybe the feeling of judgment originated from my own guilt. While we waited for results, I sang softly to Addie and fought back tears.

In the end, a spinal tap wasn't necessary. The diagnosis of Influenza A turned out to be a relief. But the doctor warned that it could still be dangerous for a newborn and that I needed to be attentive to her fluids and watch for signs of lethargy. Within two hours, I was home. Relatively simple, but terrifying.

At home, Addie and I settled back into the living room recliner. I rocked with her as she nursed and slept, nursed and slept, and her red cheeks returned to pink. At 6:30 a.m. Blake's cell phone alarm sounded its bell tone. A few minutes later he shuffled to the bathroom. When he turned on the shower, my rocking quickened and the chair began to squeak as my thoughts hissed, *He's getting up for work, not to check on us*. I listened to the floorboards creak as he made his way back to the bedroom, the groan of the closet door, the whisper of clothes, and finally the whining zip of his wool coat. Everything sounded sympathetic but him. When his shadow moved through the hall, I begged him wordlessly to come to us, place his hand on Addie's forehead, ask if we needed anything. When he didn't, I thought, *He's just going to leave, as if nothing happened*.

He paused and asked, "Are you girls going to be all right?" Eyes pinched shut, I responded. "Addie's fine."

ADDIE WAS FINE, and as her symptoms subsided, so did my anger. We closed on our new house, and as first-time homeowners, we dove into our work, ridding the three-bedroom ranch of pink and blue carpet and draperies from the 80s. The negotiation of parenting roles became a subset of tiny decisions, a lifelong process fading into more immediate decisions about cupboard hardware, paint colors, and flooring. During the weeks of remodeling, we slept at our duplex in Brookings, then Blake dropped the kids and I off at our new home in Dell Rapids on his way to work. Each day, George played, and Addie napped in her swing while I cleaned, stripped wallpaper, pulled out carpet. My mom helped patch holes in the wall after we removed a geriatric handrail from the hall. We chipped away at projects so that when Blake arrived from work, our progress was notable. Each day our home looked more like a place where a young family could settle in and begin to develop stable roots.

When it came time for floors, my cousin's husband, who had installed laminate in their house, offered tips and shared tools. With his advice, my mom and I tackled the first room—the master bedroom. By the time the screen door squealed, announcing Blake's arrival, we'd made it halfway across the room. Blake entered, stepping carefully in his black dress shoes around tools scattered over bare subfloor to where my mom and I knelt, snapping planks into place then tightening their fit with a tapping block.

"Looks good," he said. "Is it as easy as the flooring guy claimed?"

"Not quite," I admitted, "but we're getting the hang of it. You want to jump in?"

"You guys keep going," he said. "I'll watch for now."

So, mom and I finished the room, slowed by the cuts needed to fit pieces around closet walls, but proud of ourselves for not miscalculating or mis-cutting and not wasting any planks of the flooring Blake and I had spent our savings on.

When it was time to move on to the next room—George's room—Blake was ready to get involved. I was glad. I enjoyed working with my mom on projects, but this was our house, and I wanted to build it with Blake. We quickly settled into a rhythm: Blake laid out laminate planks and lined up tools, handing them to me at just the right instant. Mom complimented us. "You two make a good team."

At the end of the first row, I showed Blake how to measure and mark the plank, then led him to the chop saw set up in the garage. "So, you just line the blade up and go for it," I said, standing to the side.

Blake shook his head. "Nah, you keep cutting," he said, backing up to make space for me. "I don't want to mess things up."

"Just cut on the line. It doesn't have to be perfect. The edge will be covered up by trim."

He resisted. "You go ahead. I'll go lay out the next few pieces."

I wasn't sure if he deferred because he really thought he'd mess it up, or because he thought that this was my project. Of the two houses we considered buying, this was the one I had pushed for, with more square footage, a finished basement with cushy carpet, perfect for a playroom, a kitchen with quality cupboards, a dining room, and patio doors that opened to a fenced in back yard. "The kids can play in the yard, and I'll be able to see them from the table where I can work on my writing or the window above the kitchen sink while I cook," I'd argued. "We'd never outgrow this house." I wondered if Blake felt disconnected, somehow, like this was my house. My choice. My problem. But at the same time, I considered, maybe this was just the way our partnership worked. After all, in my parents' relationship, my mom ran the power tools too.

Whatever the case, he was in on the work. Part of the progress. And we did make a good team. It was getting dark, but we were over halfway through the third room—Addie's bedroom—and didn't want to stop until we'd finished. It seemed like a good stopping place, because it would leave only the hallway and the living room to finish up the next day. My mom offered to take the kids back to our duplex in Brookings, get them ready for bed, and we could follow whenever we were done. So, Blake and I forged ahead. An hour later, we stood in the doorway of Addie's room, admiring our work.

Blake leaned against the doorframe, and I leaned into him. "We did good, don't you think?"

"I'm a little surprised, actually," Blake said. "I think it'll look great when we put the trim back on, get the thresholds in." Bending down to pick up a scrap of floor padding, he added, "Lets clean this up a little bit before we leave."

While Blake swept, I collected spacers from along the wall, storing them on the closet shelf beside the tools we'd need to use again the next day. There, I noticed the metal heating vent we'd saved when we pulled out the carpet. I turned, saying, "I suppose we should put this back in place." I scanned the floor. "Um, Blake," I said, holding up the vent. "We forgot something,"

Blake walked to the window, pacing there, where we both knew the hole for the vent should be. "Shit," he muttered.

I exhaled a tired laugh—more disbelieving than amused.

"I'm such an idiot," Blake said. "I thought about it at one point—told myself, *don't forget to cut around the air vent*—and then we just kept going. Laid flooring right over it."

I pinched the skin between my eyes. "When we bought the house, this was the only room with blue carpet. Everything was pink, except the baby girl's room. Now it's the room without heat. This room might be jinxed."

Blake shook his head. "Nah, three-week-old baby? She doesn't need heat. She's gotta be tough enough to survive in this family of idiots."

I walked over the pristine floors to slide my arms around Blake. As proud as I'd been when we stood there just minutes before, admiring our work, I felt closer to him, hugging him tighter as we laughed at our mistake. "So, what are we idiots gonna do?"

"I don't know," he answered. "Find the vent and cut it out somehow. But first I'm going to step outside."

While Blake stood in the backyard smoking a cigarette, I called my mom. She said the kids were fine, both sleeping, and asked how the floor was coming. When I told her about the vent, she admitted, "I noticed before I left. I just didn't have the heart to say anything. You guys were working so hard, doing so good, I figured I'd wait until tomorrow when we could fix it." She suggested turning the furnace on and feeling for heat through the floor. A great idea. When Blake came in, we tried it. We heard the air rushing, and the floor beneath the window got slightly warm, but we couldn't pinpoint a spot to confidently drill through our new laminate floors. We checked the other rooms, measuring the distance between walls and vents to see if we could find a pattern. Every room was slightly different.

"If we get this wrong, we have to tear out the whole room and start over," Blake said. "I'll go downstairs and see if I can find the vent from below." He removed ceiling tiles, and after an hour of Blake and I tapping our own Morse code—him from beneath the subfloor, me from above the laminate—and one miscommunication that left a drill hole about an inch from the corner of the vent, we got it. We celebrated, sharing a beer on the dark front step, joking about how perfect we'd be for one of those home remodeling shows like *Renovations Gone Bad* or *In Over Your Head.* By the time we left, Addie's bedroom had heat. And a scarred floor. And a story we could share for the rest of our lives.

WITH FLOORS INSTALLED, we were ready to move in, just in time for me to go back to work. Since I was teaching part time, I picked the kids up from daycare in the early afternoon, which left time for cartoons or walks to the park before starting supper. Between our family meals and bedtime, we explored bike trails and riverside cliffs. Our new routine felt calm compared to the weeks of family commuting but somehow unsatisfying.

I'd fantasized about what an amazing, hands-on father Blake would be when he had the chance, but I lacked the patience to let him soothe Addie. When she cried, I wanted him to intuitively learn to hold her just so, with her stomach pressed into his chest like I did, her feet tucked under his left arm. But suggestions—"Maybe try walking around with her"—came out distorted by thoughts—*She probably doesn't want to share the spotlight with Stewie from* Family Guy. Those suggestions transformed into thinly veiled demands. "Just hold her close, like a kitten, let her cling to you." Demands became critical. "You're bouncing her too much." Then one or both of us would give up. "I'll just take her," I might say. "You and George can go play so Addie and I can rest." Or Blake might suggest, "Maybe she's hungry. Maybe you should feed her. I can't really do anything about that." I was nursing, too tired and overscheduled to pump breast milk, so responsibility fell on me.

For those first six weeks, while Blake and George snuggled under the covers of our queen-sized bed, I spent my nights in the chair with Addie, feeding her on demand, checking her breathing, never seeming to fall fully asleep. It was the same ugly chair—its thick-wale corduroy faintly stained with blood from my miscarriage and worn to strings by my feet, which I folded up under me while I worked—where I'd spent four years of mornings snuggled under a blanket with George and a pile of dinosaur books. It was the same chair I'd rocked George to sleep in when he was a baby, when I daydreamed about Blake coming home from Iraq, when I tried to imagine how nice it would be to raise a baby with a full-time, fully present husband. Then, I had filled myself with hopeful dreams of what a good dad Blake would be, of how he'd rock the baby to sleep, prepare bottles, and give me time to rest. The dreams were lighter than the air around me. Lighter than images of young men in camouflage underscored by their dates of birth and death. Lighter than local news updates on a soldier from Blake's unit, crippled by a roadside bomb. Lighter than the reality of Blake missing the first year of his son's life and the possibility of Blake never knowing his son. Those dreams saved me, elevated me, then, but now, as I snuggled in that chair with Addie, dreams morphed to expectations unmet, elevating, rising, growing further and further out of reach. While Blake and George growled battles between carnivores and herbivores downstairs or read *The Velveteen Rabbit* and *The Little Engine That Could*, I nursed Addie. I changed diapers and snapped sleepers while Blake bathed George and dressed him in baseball pajamas.

It was easy to miss as we settled into our new life, our new house, because we were so busy, but Blake felt distant. He traveled to his company's main office in Minneapolis for full weeks, sometimes, and insisted on spending weekends in Bryant so that he could hunt and farm with his brothers and dad. Something about those trips bothered me. We didn't have to go with him—we could stay in Dell Rapids, he'd be home Saturday night or Sunday—but I didn't want to spend weekends alone. So, that meant three hours of car rides each weekend with two kids. Car rides could be fun, filled with silly songs and endless rounds of "I spy with my little eye" and "I'm thinking of a dinosaur." But they could be stressful, too, Blake sometimes grew impatient with crying kids and bathroom breaks. We bought a family membership to the Children's Museum in Brookings—a stopping point halfway between Bryant and Dell Rapids—so that we could stop for a half hour to let the kids explore. And sometimes the kids drifted off to sleep, allowing the quiet, contemplative drives Blake was used to. In Bryant, the four of us slept in my upstairs bedroom at my parents' house and ate Sunday dinner at Blake's Grandma's before returning home to do laundry and prepare for a week of school and work. Our life didn't fit, exactly, with my vision of family. I'd imagined more of *us* and less of *them*. More trips to the zoo than hunting weekends.

Blake was a good dad. A hands-on dad. He developed his own baby-bouncing technique—holding Addie out in front of him, elbows at his sides, her facing away from him—which frightened me slightly but really did work. On weeknights, when Blake was home, he played Wii Sports and constructed elaborate Thomas the Train tracks with George in the basement while I cooked meals with Addie in a baby bouncer on the floor at my feet. But he never changed diapers and didn't get up at night to sooth Addie, two jobs I was more than willing to share. I wished he would connect just a bit more—a conceivable possibility, not far from our reality—but he didn't.

I wondered if this was a conscious decision, if somewhere deep down Blake didn't want to feel more connected to Addie than he had to George, or maybe he felt he was making up for lost time by focusing attention on our toddler son. That was probably wishful thinking. My gut told me it was unconscious. An unexamined but convenient deference to me, the more experienced parent. Maybe the relic of some Midwestern family values with the traditional division of domestic responsibility. I couldn't bring myself to ask, though, for fear he'd resist the questioning, or fear that the questions might disturb some delicate balance. Some part of me still feared that I could scare Blake off. That I might be too much for him. *We* might be. I heard the echo of Grandpa Dayton's question—was he fit to be a father after what he'd seen and done in war? I remembered post-deployment, re-integration advice: don't push too much on a soldier too fast.

Deployment was three years in the past, but I didn't want Blake to feel overwhelmed. Or maybe, if he felt that way, I didn't want to confront it. Or maybe it was me. Maybe I would never be satisfied. Maybe in that year of solo parenting I'd become too accustomed to doing things my way. Why did I feel the need to compare everything? Whatever the reasons, I felt, somehow, that even though Blake was there with me this time, I was still doing it alone. Unmet expectations morphed into resentment, and I drifted away from Blake, sleeping in the living room recliner every night, through the night.

It wasn't spiteful or intentional, it just happened. I told myself Addie and I slept better that way. Maybe Blake and George, who moved from his bed to ours most nights, did too. In the recliner, the warmth of Addie's body, the tickle of her breath on my neck, comforted me. I could nurse her on demand and get back to sleep more easily, but the knee of my right leg, which I always tucked under me as we rocked, began to ache, and I often woke with pinched nerves when my unsupported head tilted awkwardly. So, when Addie was six weeks old, I decided I needed better sleep. I needed to return to our bed.

I swaddled Addie, laid her in the bedside bassinet, and slipped onto the mattress beside Blake. He turned, sliding his hand over my hip, skin crackling over my fleece pajamas. When his fingers swept across my stomach, folds of skin quivered. I sucked in and instinctively rushed his hand to the sharp bone of my hip. I willed my stomach muscles to relax, but my sagging belly made me cringe. Feeling more like a mother than a wife, I wanted to lift Addie from her bassinet and retreat to the recliner. I resisted the urge, slipping my hand under Blake's to protect my soft underbelly, and fell asleep.

When something fluttered in the hallway, I woke with a gasp. I lay frozen, inhaling coarse darkness, feeling something closing in on me.

Peeling my sleep-heavy head from the pillow, I made out a shrouded shape, hanging outside the bedroom door. George's nightlight, glowing from the next room, reflected off a sunken sphere, highlighting its broad forehead and narrow, drooping chin. My breath halted. I held my body still as I listened to the wheeze, crinkle, rasp of this thing, barely audible over the inhale and exhale of the furnace.

I didn't panic, didn't register this shape as an intruder, didn't scream. It wasn't human, but it haunted me. I crept out of bed, drawn to the grotesque. As I closed in on it, the shape began to move, ducking under the door jam, levitating to the ceiling. Sagging, lifting slightly, and sagging again, it hovered there, like my own expectations, just out of reach.

I surprised myself, then, moving suddenly to grab it. The shape squealed, but quickly transformed as I made out letters, the words "It's a Girl!" printed on its Mylar face. I recognized myself in the mossy green diaper pin caved into an incongruous grin, the pallid blue bear and ashen rocking horse folded in on themselves like heavy eyelids. I shuddered at the transformation of innocence to ugliness, recalling the fruit tray and gift bags, the rattle fastened to the bottom of this helium balloon at a baby shower the previous week. I might have laughed at the realization—just a balloon, leaking helium, but I couldn't relax my pinched, angry face.

Anger. The emotion surprised me.

Clenching the tail of the balloon, I dragged it with me back to bed, where I wedged its wrinkled body beneath the frame of the mattress. I pulled the bedspread back, exposing the smooth skin of Blake's slender back as I made space for myself and crawled in. I remembered the nights, four years earlier, when George was a baby, when I slept with him beside me because Blake was gone. But now my husband was here, sleeping soundly. I knew I should be grateful. I *was* grateful. So, I allowed myself to deflate, let the expectations I'd built up for family life seep from me, let my body relax into the mattress. I leaned into Blake, stopping short of snuggling into his warmth, instead brushing the peak of his shoulder blade with my fingertips, tracing the bumps of his spine down the center of his back. I felt the tingle of fine hair on my lips as I leaned in to kiss the air just above his skin.

THE NEXT SUMMER, on a Sunday afternoon, as we drove from Bryant to Dell Rapids, I shifted in the passenger seat to face Blake. I studied his profile, steady against a blur of crabgrass, faded fence posts, rows of beans waiting for harvest, and stubbled corn fields already cut to silage. There was something I wanted to say. I wasn't sure what, exactly, but since my Grandma Evie's ninetieth birthday earlier that day, I'd been mulling over images, words, and emotions that I wanted to share with Blake. I wasn't sure how he'd react, if it would matter to him as much as it did to me, but with George and Addie already slumped in sleep in the backseat, I took a chance.

"You know my Grandpa Dayton," I said, pausing to gauge Blake's reaction. He nodded. "I saw him today. Alive and smiling. Something I never thought I'd see." Blake glanced at me from the driver's seat, lifting his chin, then looking back at the tar-veined hills of Highway 28 as he waited for my explanation. I reached across the console and placed my hand on Blake's knee while I examined the image, etched in my mind since my Aunt Martha had displayed it on her TV. "It was after you left the party today, when Martha showed Grandma her birthday present," I said. "It was an old video reel the neighbors found and put on DVD. Martha just told Grandma to watch the TV, and there he was. Grandpa Dayton." I curled and extended my fingers over the denim of Blake's jeans as I marveled. "It was amazing."

Dayton's sharp features and the recesses of his deep, narrow eyes were shadows in my line of vision, like a photo negative held up to the light. I saw Blake through that image: past layered over present, the face of the grandfather I never met cast over the husband I'd known since childhood. These two men had been connected in my mind for years—as soldiers, husbands, and fathers—but at that moment, as I marveled at a new image of my grandfather, I felt the familiar urge to understand Dayton sweep over me again.

The car hummed, tires dragging over pavement. I turned back to the landscape, letting my eyes drift along with clouds, still recreating the image of Grandpa's eyelashes fluttering, lips moving. "It wasn't even black and white," I said. "He had color in his cheeks. He was standing there with Grandma and all the kids, just grinning."

Dayton had always been a source of questions for me with Blake a source of answers. What I knew of Grandpa Dayton's story, I knew from black and white photos and the fragments of stories that sprung unexpectedly from conversation like seedlings that sprout from sidewalk cracks and landscaping. Blake knew Grandpa

Dayton only from my versions of those stories, because by the time we were married, Grandma's memory had begun to fade. And yet, Blake understood Dayton in ways I could not. Once, noticing a small black-and-white photo tucked in a china closet, Blake said, "Dayton was a first sergeant? You never told me that." I'd never told him because I hadn't known. "The patch on his uniform," Blake explained. "First Sergeant. That really meant something, especially in those days."

I'd studied that photo for years, hoping to gain some under-standing of the mysterious man who died so young, and so long before I was born. I'd memorized the slope of Grandpa Dayton's nose, the droop of his eyes, his faint smile lines. But in a glance, Blake found meaning from the photo and established a connec-tion. To Blake it was a simple, objective interpretation, and yet it mattered to him. He was connected to Dayton through me, but through military service, too. A shared history. I looked past Blake into the clear, spring sky, waves of light, split and scattered, made perceptible by dust particles and water droplets. It seemed like a dream. "I just never thought I'd see him so *happy*. I never imagined him that way, you know. All the stories about him came from Grandma Evie, and they were all sad, so I guess I just pictured him that way."

As I explained, I remembered the look on Grandma's face when she saw Dayton. She'd been smiling and shaking her head at her great grandkids, who toddled and giggled around her, when she glanced up to find the image of the husband she'd lost almost fifty years before glowing on a flat screen TV. "When she saw him, she gasped, raised her fingers to her lips, and said, 'Oh Dayt.'" She'd whispered the words so quietly I couldn't be sure I'd even heard them, but her expression was one I understood, one I'd imagined myself wearing.

When Blake was in Iraq, I worried that he might not come home and that someday his memory would catch me by surprise, leave me shaking my head in that sad, slow way like I couldn't believe such a tragedy could become distant memory and then sneak up on me. I understood Grandma's response, but I wasn't sure if Blake did. With my hand still resting on his thigh, my fingers circling his knee, I said, "Grandma used to say how hard it was when she married Baine. How she was Baine's first love, but she still loved Dayton too. She never fell out of love with him, you know, he just died."

My voice trailed off as, for a moment, Blake and I were swallowed up by a shimmering shelterbelt of cottonwood trees. I'd passed through that corridor of green thousands of times, a mile from the farm where I bottle-fed Holstein calves as a kid. The covering of trees was familiar and comforting. But that day, as Blake and I passed through its thick shade, the past hovered like low clouds—floating mist thin enough to see through, but still visible, thick enough to be felt on the skin—and I experienced the weight of their steel grey tragedy, how when Blake was a soldier in Iraq, Grandma's story of loss had shadowed the possibility of my own.

"Grandma spent her life wishing Dayton weren't gone," I said, "but loving Baine at the same time." I slid my fingers over the back of Blake's hand and tucked them against his palm. "I guess it just reminded me how glad I am that I didn't have to find out what it's like. Because while you were in Iraq, I guess I imagined the possibility."

I turned to the blur of green and blue outside my window, unable to face Blake as I confessed. "I was afraid, you know, that maybe you wouldn't come home."

My fingers were still linked with Blake's, but I felt far away from him, separated by an emotion I feared he wouldn't understand, as if my arm stretched across an ocean that divided continents not a console that divided driver and passenger seats. I'd never admitted to him how scared I was during his deployment. Instead, I'd pretended that I was as sure as he was that everything would be fine. Imagining the possibility of his death had felt like betrayal then; admitting it now felt almost as bad, but maybe that was exactly what I'd needed to say. I held my breath, waiting for Blake's response.

"I was too," he said. "I thought about it. But I guess I always believed if it happened—you know, if I didn't make it home—we'd be like them. That if you had to, you'd move on, get remarried. But I pictured it like that. That I'd be your Dayton. That it would always be me."

Blake *was* my Dayton. The twisted paths of our lives had wound us together in ways that didn't feel coincidental. Our relationship, though unpredictable, felt scripted, somehow, protected by the firmly established shelterbelts of grandparents, aunts, and uncles, their marriages proof of longevity. And as we lived our own complicated lives, our own fibrous roots extended out near the surface with sinkers diving deep to hold us steady, and leaves shedding during times of challenge, we felt connected beneath a thick canopy of family stories that would see us through difficulty to the growth that emerges each spring.

Eight

AS A YOUNG, MARRIED COUPLE, life wasn't perfect, but life was good. Healthy kids, a comfortable home, time with family. Blake's job was tolerable, his career advancing, and at least he got to work with his Uncle Les. I loved the writing I was doing as I completed my MFA, and I enjoyed teaching high school Spanish more than I'd expected. My half-time position was inching toward full time, and George had started preschool in the same building I taught in, so we moved the kids to an in-home daycare in Baltic where I could pick him up for the afternoon session. Life was fine. Better than fine, usually. We were living up to the promise Blake had asked me to make when my friend was going through a divorce—that we would never end up like that, always remember that we are on the same team—even if sometimes it felt like we were forgetting. In the morning, while I rose early to get myself ready before the kids woke, then dressed them and fed them breakfast, Blake slept. He crept out of bed with just enough time to get himself showered and out the door. If I wasn't positioned along his path from the bathroom to the garage, he might leave without ever saying a word to me. At night, he stayed up watching TV, while I read bedtime stories, usually falling asleep with the kids. When I woke, I tried to remember to join Blake on the couch for a few minutes before slipping into bed, but unless I had grading to motivate me to stay awake, I usually fell back into sleep almost instantly. We spent little time together, just the two of us, so although we worked side by side toward the same goals, we felt disconnected by divided responsibilities and conflicting routines.

One weeknight, Blake and I sat in our living room, him watching TV, me grading student papers while I wrestled with news I'd received that day at school: one of my students had attempted suicide. Each scribble of handwriting, each students' name reminded me, and questions resurfaced. Feeling the familiar need to make sense of things through conversation, I confided in Blake.

"I still can't believe it," I said. "And I know I'm not supposed to talk about it, but you don't know these people, and I just can't stop thinking about it, so I have to tell you. One of my students tried to kill himself." I turned to Blake, shaking my head in disbelief. "Can you believe that? A smart kid, kind of quiet, but from a good family, and he just doesn't think he can handle things." I felt unsettled.

This student was so much like all the others, walking into class each day in jeans and T-shirt, backpack slung over his shoulder, smiling. He was a bookworm, slightly introverted, but not an outcast. He was absent a lot—I'd noticed that—but so smart, earning As on tests without studying. And then, suddenly, he was gone for two weeks. When he returned, he hinted at the reason for his absence telling me maybe I should talk to the counselor, so I'd know what happened. When I followed up, the counselor was glad he was opening up to someone, so she filled in details of his multiple suicide attempts.

Sparing Blake the details, I simply said, "He thinks life is so bad he doesn't want to live. It just doesn't seem like he should feel like he has to, I don't know, like he doesn't have . . . " I was fumbling. I'd felt compelled to tell Blake, hoping I would find words or understanding in the process. He was usually a willing listener, even if he didn't offer answers. But that night he flipped through channels, almost seeming not to hear me. I stared at him, my frustration growing, until, finally, he spoke.

"Yeah," he nodded. "Kids do stupid things."

I squinted my eyes, jutted my chin toward him, dumbfounded by what I read as callousness. "How can you say that? What do you mean, stupid? He's just a kid."

"Exactly, kids are stupid." Blake shrugged, "They do stupid things."

I exhaled audibly. Blake could be this way sometimes, sort of flippant about people's problems. This was the disconnected Blake, the part of him I felt I could never quite reach, the part I could never bring myself to engage or question. When someone was diagnosed with cancer, he might say, "Yeah, it's sad, but he's lived a good life. Has a good family. Nobody lives forever." And while I agreed in some ways with the futility of wallowing in sadness, I believed in compassion. Sometimes I appreciated Blake's ability to stay grounded, to resist wide-swaying emotion, but sometimes I wanted him to just *feel*. Feel sorry for someone. Sympathize with a teenage kid who had attempted suicide. That night, I pushed back. "Blake, that's a terrible thing to say. He's just a kid."

"Yeah, I know," he said, as if we were seeing eye-to-eye. "He's just a kid. Doesn't know any better. So, he did something stupid. That's what I mean. Kids do stupid things."

I gave up. My eyes fell back to the homework on my lap as I shook my head, Blake's words rattling there. On the couch, Blake went quiet, too, returning his attention to the TV, I assumed. A familiar jingle, which I usually couldn't help but hum along to, aggravated me. "*It seems today that all you see is violence in movies and sex on TV.*" I shuffled my papers, preparing to retreat to the bedroom, when suddenly, Blake chuckled. I jerked my head toward the TV, prepared to roll my eyes at cartoon antics, but the screen faded from one commercial to the next. Blake stared at the rug. Confused, I leaned in his direction. Then silence gave way, like a trap door.

"You know, there was this kid who offed himself in a porta-john," Blake said.

The words—*offed himself, porta-john*—dropped into our living room, where they lay between us like a grenade, its pin still intact with the potential for detonation implied but not imminent. I held my breath as I asked, "What are you talking about?"

'In Baghdad," he said, pointing the remote reflexively at the TV, chuckling again. I recognized the sinister laugh, deep and muffled, shaking inside the mass of his body without escaping. Blake hadn't told any war stories in a long time, but I recognized this as the posture, the voice, of those stories. I braced myself, but my exasperation softened.

"Did you know him?" I asked.

Blake scrolled through the TV menu aimlessly. "No, I didn't know him at all, actually. Don't even know his name. But we were doing those night missions, sleeping during the day. So, I was asleep one morning, woke up to the sound of a gunshot, but you heard stuff like that all the time, so I didn't think anything of it." Still paging through programs, he went on. "I got up to go to the bathroom, and there was a bunch of guys cleaning the johns. I wondered what those guys did to deserve that, you know. That was a real shit job. The Iraqi's usually did it." Another chuckle. "Turned out they were cleaning up the kid's mess." He spoke as if in a trance, his voice soft, a vulnerable underbelly, protected beneath a hard shell of laughter.

Feeling the need to respond, I offered the only words I could find. "That's terrible."

"Yeah, it really is," Blake said. "And later, I remember talking to Serna about it, because it bothered me. It made me mad, actually." His voice rose as he went on. "I mean, why would you kill yourself in the worst place in the world," Blake asked, "when you know that all you have to do is say one word, just mention that—that you want to die—and they'll send you home? The Army doesn't want this stuff to happen. They'd rather get a guy outta there than have stuff like that going on. All he had to do was say it, and he was home."

Anger rattled Blake's head from side to side. Then he paused. "But Serna had a pretty good point—what if home was the problem? What if the kid wanted out of Iraq but home wouldn't be any better?" Blake nodded sympathetically. "And then it was like, yeah, you never know the whole story."

Finally, I understood. Blake was asking the same question as me, wondering how a kid's life could seem that bad, and how suicide could seem like the only answer. But while I whispered in the soothing voice of a mother and wife, a nurturing teacher, Blake barked in the practical, detached tone of a soldier with the sarcastic bite of dark humor.

I examined that misunderstanding and realized that in so many ways, I still didn't know my husband. There were parts of him I hadn't touched. I wondered if I ever could. But it felt hopeful too. As a teacher, I knew that learning takes place outside our comfort zones. If we could face that discomfort in the muted, safe space of our living room with our kids sleeping down the hall, we could learn together, become better. The dark room suddenly felt brighter, like the day I came home from work to find the large evergreen in our front yard cut down. When we bought the house, Blake had identified it right away as something that needed to go, even though he was a tree lover and hated to cut them down. It was overgrown, encroaching on the driveway, touching the siding of the garage, and once it was gone, the whole street felt sunny. Neighbors gathered on the sidewalk, smiling, waving, and joking, "Now I can spy on you from my front porch!" and planning a block party. It's amazing how things change when light shines in.

"So," Blake said. "Kids are stupid. Kids do stupid things."

"Yeah," I said. "Sometimes we just get too far in, can't see any way out."

"Yeah, or sometimes we're just stupid," he said. Now I smiled at the way he toed the line of insensitivity. This was the stubborn debater, Blake. The one who challenged my interpretations of the novels I read in college English classes, just for fun. I reached to set aside my students' papers, preparing to move beside Blake, place my hand on his knee, but before I could stand, he was talking again.

"There was another time too. We were on station, ready for a mission, when they called and said they had to go one hundred percent, accounting for everybody." Blake had stopped pretending to search for programs. The screen glowed, and he stared ahead, but not at me, not at the TV. "Serna came around, checking everybody. He had to actually physically see each one and check them in, because this kid at the FAB down the road just went crazy—jumped the fence and took off running, in his PT gear." Blake's laugh was lighter, closer to the surface this time, giving me hope that maybe this was actually a funny story, not a "funny" war story. "Some guys were driving around and found him running down the deal, you know, down the road. Caught him and brought him back."

I pictured a kid in black shorts, a gray T-shirt with ARMY printed across the chest, scampering down a dusty road, a handful of uniformed soldiers tackling him. At least he was alive at the end of the story. But before I could assess whether this was actually amusing, Blake shook his head. "Stupid kids," he said again.

"They weren't the only ones, though," he went on. "We all did stupid things. So many things you look back on and think, that's ridiculous, the way you did things, almost trying to get yourself killed, knowing you had no business doing things that way." The steady cadence of Blake's voice, the way one story morphed into another was both comforting and concerning. I savored the outpouring, but I couldn't help but wonder what would come next, and wished for a moment to tread water, collect my thoughts, and catch my breath.

Blake stood, then, and moved toward the picture window. He pulled back a thin curtain and looked out into the dark before he let it fall back into place as he turned to me. "They have these color codes for all the roads according to how dangerous they are." He paced. "It changes all the time—one week a street is coded red, the next week green—but there were some places that you knew you were never supposed to go." He shook his head at the memory, "I remember the last weeks. We were just about ready to go home, so you know, guys knew pretty damn well where the bad spots were. And then the one day, Serna gives us directions to the airport, the route we should take, and we all laugh, thinking, this isn't the way we're going, thinking he's messing with us."

His voice slowed. "And it's like, 'Yeah, this is the only way we can go.' We look at him, tell him he's crazy, but Serna's like, 'I know, but it's the only way.'" Blake sat back on the couch, perching close to the edge of the cushion, his head shaking, his upturned palms bobbing under the weight of inevitability. "And we all know, it's like we're begging to get killed. You tell yourself, 'You're gonna die doing that.' But that's the way that deal goes. You don't have a choice."

I was speechless. Blake grew quiet too. He felt closer to me, more exposed than he'd ever been, but more distant, too. When his face and muscles relaxed, when he returned to flipping through channels, I moved next to him on the couch. "Thanks," I whispered, as he lifted his arm, inviting me to rest against him. "Thanks for telling me that." I hoped he understood my words to mean, "You can always tell me anything."

As silence stretched out, a question surfaced. I'd been wondering for years about the funny war story Blake told me over the phone while he was in Iraq. Now seemed like the time to ask. "So, this is probably a stupid question, and you don't have to answer," I started in, "but remember when you told me about the Iraqi policeman with a hole in his guts? How he got up and walked home?" Blake laughed and nodded. "You said that was a funny war story, but I've never understood why you would say that."

Blake lifted his arm from around my shoulder. As his posture stiffened, I straightened myself on the couch next to him, regretting the question that seemed to separate us again. But he turned to look me in the eye as he explained. "It's funny because that's just how ridiculous things were. The ambulance was on its way. We could hear the sirens. But this poor guy was more afraid of an ambulance ride across Baghdad, the only thing that might have saved him, than of walking home to die."

It still didn't strike me as funny, but at least now it made some sort of sense as a Catch-22. I nodded to show that his explanation satisfied me. Blake lifted his arm and pulled me close, and I settled in, content with our progress.

GEORGE WAS IN FIRST GRADE when I noticed his own questions surfacing as he explored the complexities of naming, linking big words with wide reaching meanings like soldier, war, and veteran, with the little word he had understood so easily. Dad.

George had seen pictures of Blake in uniform from the welcome home, and whenever we happened to drive down Marion Road in Sioux Falls, he knew which apartment complex to point to, knew to say, "That's the first place we lived. Me and mom. When Dad was gone." He giggled about it, like it was our little secret, a whole year that was just his and mine. I tried to ensure that his dad's military service wasn't a secret, talk about it just enough that George would know he could ask questions. One day, as he colored at his desk after school, George did just that. "When I was born, my dad was gone, because he was in the Army, right?"

I turned to see the cap of George's sandy blonde hair as he leaned over his paper. "Yep. He was far away. In Baghdad."

"So, what was he doing there?" George asked.

"Training Iraqi policemen," I said. Hoping to satisfy his curiosity and avoid questions I might not be able to answer, I added, "His job was to teach them how to protect their country."

In the silence that followed, I moved toward George, trying to imagine some satisfactory answer for some difficult question, but George let me off the hook. "So, my dad is a soldier?"

"He was," I said, reaching out to tousle his hair. "He's not in the Army anymore, though." I crouched down and pulled his body into mine for a quick hug.

"So now he's called a veteran," he said, "like Veterans Day." He pulled back to check my expression, his eyebrows raised.

"That's right," I nodded, leaning in to kiss his forehead. "We're lucky he's home with us now, aren't we?" I punctuated the conversation with another quick hug that tugged George's cheek up toward my shoulder then returned to my work.

A few days later, George's winning entry from the elementary school's Veterans Day coloring contest came home in his folder. Pulling it out, I was immediately struck by George's choice of image. I'd seen collages of the pictures hanging around school, so

I knew that students had chosen between a handful of images: a group of soldiers in a tidy line presenting the colors, the Iwo Jima flag raising, or a stoic soldier poised in front of a flag. George chose the single soldier.

I studied the meticulously colored uniform, the splashes of gold and red George used to embellish medals and bars, surprised that a seven-year-old boy would choose this erect posture and solemn face over the action of the other images. When I realized how the posture reminded me of my Grandpa Dayton, and the photo I'd studied for years as I tried to fill in the gaps of his story, it made sense. To George, a soldier was not an action figure or a movie star. When George thought of soldiers, he thought of his dad. As I studied the stripes of the flag George had colored—not bleeding into one another, but distinct, crisp lines—I imagined George, replaying our conversation while formulating questions about his dad's military service as he concentrated on the pressure of his fingers, and paused to dust away flakes of wax with a puff of warm breath, the sweep of a hand. His choice of image was calculated and significant. He'd taken great care with his coloring. It meant something to him.

The significance became evident again a few weeks later, when we browsed Christmas ornaments in a craft store. From the aisles of sparkly, sporty, rustic, and every imaginable kind of ornament, George picked a kneeling soldier with his hat pulled down over his eyes. "I think we should have this ornament for our tree. For my dad." The soldier had dark skin and black hair, but the uniform and the solemn posture represented his dad.

George was always good at linking things. As a toddler, he easily linked words into sentences, lines into shapes and figures, and bikes and trailers into a makeshift train. Even as a baby, he connected things—me to Blake's family during deployment, all of us to memories of his dad and hope for the future. On the day of Blake's homecoming, George skipped the furrowed-brow stare that he usually offered strangers and settled comfortably into his father's arms. And within the first year after Blake returned from war, George made the bond official, declared it, by balancing next to him on the couch, placing his arm over Blake's shoulder, and saying, "We are friends."

I had worried that George might not feel that connection, that he might need time to develop and trust that relationship, but he'd seemed to understand. Now he seemed to intuit how deeply the experience of being a soldier and going to war affected his dad. He seemed to appreciate the significance of that part of his identity but also its complexity. George linked military service to stoicism and solemnity. Maybe we were all beginning to piece together the connection between Blake's late nights on the couch, his slow rising in the morning and the physical pain and mental strain of that part of his identity.

WHEN I WENT TO THE KITCHEN to put away my laptop one night after reaching the bottom of a mound of student essays, Blake followed me. The kids had been sleeping for hours, and I was ready to join them, ready to rest up for another day of work.

"So, I had an appointment at the VA today," Blake said.

"That's right," I said, resting my hand on the counter. "So did you finally get the results from your MRI?"

"I did," he said. "They still don't want to do surgery, so that's good." He nodded, as if to spur the conversation on, which surprised me. This wasn't a topic he usually brought up.

"I guess so," I said, "but do they have any treatment options?"

"Some new pills," he said, shrugging. "A sleeping pill, too, this time."

"A sleeping pill?" I asked. "Why?"

"Because I can't sleep," he teased.

For months, Blake, the kids and I had been playing what I called musical beds. Sometime after midnight, the sound of small hands fumbling with a doorknob, the plod of tired feet over laminate flooring signaled that Addie needed comfort. After flipping a blanket or two, at least one pacifier, and often a bald baby doll or stuffed animal onto the mattress, she would climb in and roll her body over mine, landing in the soft ditch between Blake and I. A few hours later, George would follow, lifting the covers on my side of the bed and snuggling into my chest. Usually, when I woke between four and six in the morning, I'd find Blake's side of the bed empty, him curled in the soft red fleece of our living room blanket or in Addie's single bed. I'd assumed his part in this game of bed switching was just an escape from the heat of too many bodies, the sharp knees and elbows of our kids. Now, I faced a revision of this nighttime ritual as a sign of silent suffering. "You mean, you can't sleep because of your back?"

Blake nodded, then surprised me by adding, "You know, I've decided, I'm gonna get my disability reevaluated. Get whatever documents I need, go for whatever I can get."

His sudden willingness sounded an alarm. I remembered my mom commenting on Blake's walk—the strange stiffness of his torso, the motion of his legs limited by the awkward angle—and how it made her want to cry, seeing him in so much pain. That was almost a year ago, I thought, wanting to cry myself as I realized how normal it had become to see him that way, and how bad it must actually be if he was finally willing to talk. Over the years, when I shoveled snow because Blake's back hurt too bad, I'd complained. *"You know, we could buy a snowblower with disability money."* Now I felt guilty. "You're thirty-three years old, and you need a sleeping pill to get through the night. What's it going to be like when you're fifty? Do you worry about that?"

"Yeah, it's awfully disappointing," Blake said. "But it is what it is. That's why I've decided to do it—get my disability reevaluated."

"So, what do we do?" I asked.

"Paperwork," he laughed, "and take sleeping pills, I guess."

By summer, it was clear increased pain meds and sleeping pills weren't enough, and Blake was referred to the VA in Omaha, Nebraska, for a surgical consult. The news came as a relief to him, because although he'd been warned by friends to put off back surgery for as long as he could, he needed relief. On one weekend visit to Bryant, he'd forgotten his shaving kit with all his medicine in it, and he insisted on driving almost two hundred miles round trip rather than go without it for the night. He complained to me, "I'm barely thirty years old, and I can't stand for five minutes. I have to sit down to put on my shoes. I have to sit on the toilet to brush my teeth." These were no longer minor inconveniences. This was life, disrupted.

Blake was chipper when he told me about the appointment. "We'll pack a lunch, then after the VA, we'll go to the zoo. Make it a family day."

I couldn't argue with that. We'd taken the kids to the Omaha Zoo the summer before, and Blake enjoyed it as much as they did, quizzing George about the difference between llamas and alpacas, chimps and monkeys. The day of the appointment, I packed a cooler full of sandwiches and juice boxes and we headed south on I-29 at 5 a.m. The kids slept most of the way, so I read and napped while Blake drove. When we hit the edge of the city, I read the directions I'd printed out from Google Maps, and we pulled into the parking lot of the VA. George stirred, asking if we were almost to the zoo, but Addie stayed asleep.

"You guys don't have to come in," Blake said, as he unbuckled his seatbelt. My initial reaction was surprise, but as soon as he said it, it made sense. Two kids in a medical consultation could be a little distracting. Besides, I'd offered many times to go to appointments with him. He'd always declined.

"We could just sit in the waiting room," I offered.

"No, don't worry about it. We don't need to make the kids walk all the way up there." As he motioned to the building, I realized he'd parked in the second lot, further from the hospital. "And besides, VA hospitals can be kind of depressing." I conceded with a nod. I'd never actually been inside one, but George had visited other hospitals and always left overwhelmed.

"I'll just give the kids some breakfast, but you can call if you want us to come in—if it's taking a while, or if you need me for anything."

Blake nodded, and I wished him luck. With time to kill, I roused Addie from sleep and changed her diaper. I unpacked peanut butter and jelly sandwiches and poked straws into juice boxes. Then, just as I considered walking George up to the bathroom, Blake surprised me by opening the car door. He'd barely been gone ten minutes.

"Did you forget something?" I asked. "Some paperwork?" I pictured him, turned away at the check-in for some unprocessed referral, a missing insurance card.

"Nope," he said, shutting the door and making his way to the rear of the car, where he lit a cigarette. I jumped out, confused.

As Blake paced, questions buzzed— Did we come on the wrong day? Was his appointment rescheduled and we didn't know?—but before I could ask, Blake exhaled a puff of smoke. "He said I'm too young for surgery." His voice rumbled. "I have to sit on the toilet to brush my teeth, and I'm too young for surgery. I'm in pain constantly, and I feel like I could just snap. All the time. At work. At home. But I'm too young for surgery."

Our car was parked beneath a row of trees, protected from the rising July sun, but it felt like we were shrouded in ominous clouds. I wanted to wrap my arms around Blake to comfort him, but he seemed inconsolable.

I asked, "What does that mean? Too young for surgery?"

Blake was so upset that words tumbled from him. I struggled to keep up. "It wouldn't last, he said, and they can only do this surgery once, or, I don't know, he just said my pain isn't bad enough to justify it now, at this age." He mumbled something about an orthopedic surgeon and neurological surgeon. I wished I'd been in the appointment, wished I understood. The only thing I knew was that this was worse than I'd imagined. Blake was desperate.

He dropped his cigarette, digging his toe into the ground to stub it out. "I'm just glad you guys are here. If I'd have driven down here alone, for this? I'd be awfully God damned pissed." I couldn't help but smile at the way he sounded like his Grandpa Bob with that strange string of expletives. And at the fact that having us with him somehow helped. "Let's go to the zoo," he said. "Get something good out of this trip."

A MONTH LATER, back at the Sioux Falls VA, I sat in the corner of an exam room on a curved plastic chair—the kind that cups your body, giving the illusion of comfort. An entire wall of the doctor's office might have been made up of windows—lower panes frosted for privacy, upper panels clear, allowing light in—and yet the room seemed clouded. Maybe the day was overcast, maybe the room had fewer windows than I remember. Or maybe it was guilt or regret or fear that cast a shadow. But at least I was there. The fact that Blake had asked me to come with him was a sign of light coming in, even if, when we entered the exam room, Blake took the chair next to the doctor's workstation, rather than sliding up onto the examination table, relegating me to the corner. I peered across the room, watched Blake's eyes graze the floor.

"You can be honest," I said, leaning toward him, hoping he would look up. "You have to be honest. You deserve to feel better."

Blake acknowledged me with a glance, and then the physician's assistant entered. She took her place on a padded, swiveling stool, her back to me, greeted Blake, and moved into the initial questions. I felt like I was eavesdropping. "Any feelings of depression?" A quick no. "Thoughts of hurting yourself?" Another negative. I nodded in agreement. And then she asked, "How many alcoholic beverages do you consume in a week?" Blake probably answered honestly—sometimes one or two on a weeknight, on the weekend sometimes four or five. She seemed unconcerned. "So, how are you doing overall, Blake?"

He responded without hesitation. "Not that well, actually." He paused.

In that sliver of silence, I prepared to interject, explain that it wasn't just golf or baseball, or not being able to shovel snow. That Blake couldn't stand without swaying and pacing. He was losing flexibility, his feet heavy stumps. He couldn't sleep. I leaned forward, preparing to move around the wall created by this woman's body, but as I ran through the symptoms in my head—some I had only recently learned of myself—I realized that maybe Blake needed this wall between us, maybe he didn't need to feel me examining his weakness. So, I shrank into my plastic chair and listened. When Blake spoke, he didn't recite a list of symptoms. "We've tried all these treatments," he said, "but it just keeps getting worse." He forced out words. "I really don't know how long I can live like this."

I closed my eyes to absorb words I hadn't heard him speak before and to face the desperation I had sensed mounting but never confronted. I remembered Blake's high school friend stopping by to offer us life insurance. Was that a coincidence? Grandpa Dayton and Grandma Evie flashed in my memory. How many times had she told me Dayton always believed he would die young? How often had she repeated his insistence on life insurance, "Because a man needs to take care of his family, even if—especially if— something happens to him." I remembered her words, now feeling them as my own desperate cry: "Oh Dayt, you're not going to die." I wanted to crawl across the room, kneel on the floor beneath Blake's downturned eyes and plead with him. "You don't have to live like this, we'll find something to make you feel better. We're not going to lose you. Stay with me." But as words, memory, and fear trembled in my body, the PA moved on cheerfully.

She drew her shoulders back, positioned her glasses, and flipped through the pages of Blake's file. "Well, let's see what we can do, then. We've tried physical therapy." I imagined Blake's eyes rolling back, his jaw clenching in frustration at the reminder of years of therapy with no benefits. "We've done cortisone," she added. I imagined the muscles of Blake's core tightening, his body stiffening at the memory of months between shots, the insistence that sometimes it takes a few tries before cortisone provides relief. Still flipping pages, the PA said, "I see image guided cortisone, no success there. And the surgical consult?" She peered at him over her glasses, waiting for a response.

Blake exhaled. "It was a joke. Lasted five minutes." His voice was tight and sharp, pinching back the same anger I'd heard in July when he was assessed as "too young for surgery."

The PA returned to Blake's file, saying, "Well, then, let's see what we can do to manage that pain." She thumbed back and forth. "We can't go any higher on hydrocodone, so it looks like the next step would be morphine."

Her tone was steady, the word morphine uttered as easily as Tylenol, linking seamlessly to a memorized explanation of schedule I drugs and possession of controlled substances. I felt the word on my skin. *Morphine.* Hairs on my arms raised. My skin crawled like it had when I was thirteen with morphine dripping into my veins after back surgery, when I thought snakes slithered around me in my bed and up my arms, and I imagined men on stilts teetering in the corner of my hospital room. Too young for surgery. "Don't know how long I can live." Morphine. Words rolled and rumbled like fast motion images of storm clouds gathering.

I didn't know at the time that the hydrocodone Blake had been taking for years was just as bad as morphine, that it, too, bound itself to opiate receptors, essentially tricking the brain into feeling intense pleasure, but then losing effect leading to increased tolerance, decreased effectiveness. I didn't know, then, that the VA's opiate prescriptions were rising drastically faster than their number of patients, that their fatal overdose rate was rising to almost twice the national average. But I did know that stories of homeless, alcoholic, drug-addicted veterans were suddenly more immediate and more real to me. Just hearing the word morphine had given me a terrifying understanding of how easily that could become our story. I wanted to claw my way past the PA, clench Blake's shoulders, and look into his eyes, search for signs of life, signs that he wasn't disappearing into this possibility.

One word—*morphine*—convinced me that Blake was bound by a VA medical system that was failing him, tricking him, numbing him into believing that all he needed was pain management. A higher dosage. Another drug. And I'd missed it. I felt disoriented, as I had standing at the top of Costa Rica's Arenal volcano, where

I was swallowed in thick fog. I'd climbed that mountain, so I knew that somewhere was a wooden walkway with chipped green paint, one I'd just walked over to reach the platform, that there was a railing nearby that I could feel for and eventually find with the hand that seemed not to exist when I extended it in front of me. But I also knew that beyond the railing was the crater of a volcano. I knew there was a safe way out of that fog, that if I needed to, I could drop to my knees and crawl over splintered wood until I found smooth pavement. But I sensed that deep cavity below, the danger of possibility. In the exam room of the VA hospital, I closed my eyes to the disorienting scene and began to feel for something that might steady me. I clenched the metal frame of my plastic chair. Remembering my research into treatments for degenerative disk disease—inversion tables, implants, surgeries—I said, "There has to be something else you can do."

The PA faced Blake as she explained, "There's really nothing else we can do for you here, though you may find help with an orthopedic surgeon." There was a catch. "Unfortunately, I can't make the referral," she said. "We have an orthopedic surgeon on staff, so I can't refer you to an outside provider, even though our surgeon doesn't deal with spinal injury. It's policy. We can't refer out for services we offer internally."

Maybe she turned to Blake thinking that only he—the veteran, the insider—would understand the complexity. But I had read *Catch-22* too. Blake was trapped by policy. What I didn't understand was why this treatment had never been mentioned before, or why a system paying a veteran for his disability would want to prolong that disability rather than eliminate it. I moved to the edge of my chair. "But you're saying there is treatment available outside the VA?"

Still answering to Blake, the PA offered, "If I were you, yes, I would see what else is available. It does appear to be an orthopedic problem. You would, of course, be on your own financially."

When Blake spoke, I expected an objection. Instead, he laughed. It was the incredulous laugh of Yossarian, recognizing absolute simplicity, or a trapped animal, acknowledging the metal teeth sunken into its flesh, the necessity of gnawing its own leg off to save itself. "I guess I have to thank you, really. I just wish someone had told me five years ago."

The PA spun toward her computer, fingers skipping over keys as she summarized the visit. She spun back. "So, Blake, I'm going to go ahead and send these prescriptions." She maintained an even tone, professional detachment, recapping, "When you get downstairs, you'll need to sign some paperwork since this new prescription is a controlled substance, but the pharmacist will explain it all again." Did she feel satisfied? I wondered. Relieved at the possibility that Blake might finally receive the care he needed? Or maybe she felt a tinge of regret, knowing that he should have received that care years ago, or guilt, knowing that we would end up paying out-of-pocket for the treatment of this service-related disability. Did she worry about what might happen to a young father and husband, about what might happen to his family, if he became dependent on the morphine she prescribed?

I didn't have time to consider. I was already searching for an orthopedic surgeon on my phone. In the waiting room, I dialed the Orthopedic Institute. They offered an appointment later in the week. I tugged at Blake's forearm, pulling him toward me, begging. "Don't fill the prescription, please. It's only a few days." I slipped my hand down his arm, laced my fingers with his. "You can last a few days, right?"

Blake squeezed my hand. A low laugh escaping as he said, "Yeah, morphine is like the last hope of a dying man." His fingers fell from mine, and he turned away as he said, "Anyway, I have to fill the other prescriptions, so I'll meet you at home."

The good news was that Blake's pain had finally mounted to a point where it demanded attention. Chandelier pain. A spot so sensitive that touching it sends the sufferer to the ceiling. No more laughing away symptoms. No more coping and getting by, relying on remedies that have worked in the past. No more sleepwalking through life. The problem became so obvious that we had no choice but to find a solution.

The solution came less than two weeks after the VA appointment, when Blake checked in to the Orthopedic Institute for a microdiscectomy. A nurse led us to his room, but before we entered, she pulled me aside. She handed me the gallon zip-top bag full of Blake's prescriptions, which we had brought, as instructed.

"Thank you for bringing these in," she said politely. Then she glanced over her shoulder, as if checking for eavesdroppers, as she asked. "Does your husband really take all these?"

I raised my eyebrows. "I guess so. I mean, yes, I think they're all current." There were regular pain meds, as-needed pain meds, others for high blood pressure. "Maybe some are old, I don't know."

She cut me off. "Well, please, take these home." Her hands fluttered. "And I would suggest disposing of as many as you can." I stuffed the bag into my purse as she added, "Hopefully, he won't need them after the procedure." I nodded, feeling ashamed for not knowing what exactly was in that bag, wondering how I was supposed to "dispose" of it. I left that question for later, since Blake was already emerging from the bathroom in a hospital gown.

Within an hour, a nurse came to tell me everything had gone well and to lead me to the recovery room. I entered to find Blake, smiling.

"I suppose it's not really possible," he said. "It's probably the drugs talking, but I swear I feel better." In spite of the blue-print smock, the IV taped to his arm, the white sheet tucked around his lower body—the usual signs of sickness and fragility—Blake beamed. "I don't think there's pain in my leg, and my back hurts, but it's different, like no more pressure, like it's a good pain."

The relief was visible. I marveled at the way his smile reached his eyes. Since I left him, hardly an hour earlier, he had transformed, not into someone new, but someone familiar. The sincere, shy boy I'd studied for years, the poised athlete I'd laughed with in the dugout, the confident, teasing, intelligent man I'd fallen in love with over book discussions and long, ambling drives. How long had it had been since I'd seen that smile?

Years. I'd forgotten it even existed.

Now, he looked young and sincerely happy. Reborn.

I felt happy, too—my cheeks aching from my own atrophied smile—but guilty. My stomach tightened. How had I not noticed the absence of that smile?

When we checked out of the hospital, they handed Blake a prescription for less than half the dose of hydrocodone he'd been on for years. The nurse explained, "To be clear, you shouldn't drive while taking this."

In the elevator, Blake laughed. "I can't drive? I've been taking twice that much, all that other stuff, and the VA never mentioned anything about driving."

The light of realization ignited. "Because then you would have been one hundred percent disabled."

AT HOME, BLAKE MOVED SLOWLY, walking only blocks, at first, but within days he had picked up the pace and was walking miles, sleeping soundly. When he rose from the couch and slipped into the jeans he kept folded on the floor beside him, then laced his tennis shoes, I teased. "You could wear sweatpants, you know. Or athletic shorts. It can't be comfortable to walk in jeans."

"I'm not wearing gym clothes unless I'm at a gym," he explained. "I don't wear sweatpants in public."

"But you're walking. That's exercise."

He rolled his eyes. As an athlete, he'd never considered walking exercise. "You walk on the golf course, too, but you don't see anyone golfing in gym shorts. It's basic human decency."

I wanted to tease him about his country club rules, but laughed, instead, as he made his way out into the cool fall morning in his jeans. The fact that he laughed so easily now signaled that he was returning to life. When he woke each morning, he rose effortlessly, as if eager to start the day. I remembered his slow mornings over the previous years, recognized them as now signs of chronic pain, thinking how long ago he could have begun this return. But mostly I relished the fact that life seemed easier now.

One day, as I swept the living room, I overheard a conversation between Blake and Addie. She was potty training and still required assistance, so nothing seemed out of the ordinary, until I heard her singsong voice ask, "Daddy, does your back feel better now?" I swept my way closer to the hall and paused, listening for Blake's answer.

"Yeah," he sounded genuinely relieved. "It does feel better."

I pictured her enthusiastic nod, shaking the loose curls around her face. "So, does that mean you can carry me now?" I closed my eyes to a twinge of regret: even Addie had catalogued the signs of her dad's suffering.

Blake chuckled. "Yeah, I guess it does. I can carry you now, but still not too much. Pretty soon I'll carry you all the time."

A pause followed, and I pictured her chubby cheeks scrunched into a cheesy smile. Then she finalized the conversation. "Good.

So, now, can you wipe my butt?" Addie's giggle highlighted a sense of giddy relief. Each day, we laughed more, Blake walked further, longer. He was getting better. I thought the danger had passed.

But then, one afternoon about a month after surgery, I noticed Blake pacing the living room. He perched momentarily on the couch, his face red, neck sweating, then rose and circled the rug. He sat again, then paced. He spoke in spasms. "I feel awful. You know, I thought it was great. I thought the surgery worked. And now I feel terrible."

"Maybe you need to take a walk," I offered. He'd returned to work, just a few hours a day. "Maybe it's all the sitting. A walk will help."

Blake walked, but he didn't eat supper. I shooed the kids downstairs and entertained them until bedtime, sensing that Blake couldn't handle even happy noise. He went to bed early. When I joined him, he moved to the couch. Snap of a blanket, shuffling pillows, then silence. These were warning signals I'd missed before. Now they screamed trouble. I held my breath. More shuffling, the squeal of skin against leather. I went to check on him. "What's wrong, Blake? What do you need?"

He spoke in tight, choked phrases. "I don't know. I can't sleep. I don't think it worked. The surgery. I think it's worse than before."

I was on my knees beside the couch, my hand on his shoulder. "I can sleep here. The bed is probably better for your back." I ran my hand over the fleece he'd pulled up over his head. He grunted. I gave up and returned to bed.

Unable to sleep, I stared at the ceiling, making out shapes in the dark—the plant hook left from the previous owner, the light fixture we'd always planned to replace with a ceiling fan. When I closed my eyes, I remembered Blake's pacing, fidgeting. For a month, he'd felt so good. How could things go so suddenly wrong?

Why did he seem so nervous? Agitated. As I catalogued symptoms, a connection fired. I reached for my iPhone and, angling the blinding screen away from my eyes, opened the internet browser and typed: *hydrocodone symptoms of withdrawal*. The results: sweating, nausea, phantom pain. Remembering Blake's red face, his clammy skin, his pacing, I wanted to run to him, reassure him, "It's not the surgery. Your back is fine. You're just addicted to drugs." He would appreciate the dark humor. But he was sleeping, or at least quiet, so I waited until morning.

When Addie stirred in her bed, early, as always, I finally had an excuse to wake Blake. I offered him a choice—good news or bad news. He opted for good news, so I said, "I don't think it's the surgery. I don't think that's what's bothering you." I paused. "The bad news is, I think you're addicted to hydrocodone." When I handed him the list of symptoms, he laughed and shook his head.

"I guess it's kind of a relief."

Laughter was the best we could do, but he was still agitated and sweating, and by the time he called the VA later in the morning, he was dry heaving too. "They've had me on this medicine for years, never mentioned addiction. And now I call them for help, because I want to get off it, and now they treat me like an addict." He yanked his shoelaces into a tight knot. "They won't do anything until Monday. I have to come in for an emergency appointment." He stood, head jerking side to side, hands on hips. "So, I guess I'm going for a walk."

"But you're coming home, right? You're not gonna go live under a bridge or anything?" We both laughed again—mine a nervous question that shivered through my body, Blake's a loud rumble trapped in his clenched jaw.

"I'll be home," he said. "But if not, at least you know where to start looking."

BLAKE DID COME HOME, and addiction didn't overcome him, but he wrote off the VA forever. On Monday, he called the Orthopedic Institute. They prescribed him enough hydrocodone to taper off, one pill per day for two weeks, then a half, then a half every other day. Instead of searching for my husband under a bridge, I watched him continue his return to life.

Hope renewed, Blake embraced the promise that life could be better than it had been, seeking out a new job that might offer more fulfillment, and an opportunity to relocate from Dell Rapids closer to home. Blake accepted and started a job selling insurance in De Smet, just seventeen miles from our hometown of Bryant, so we prepared for another move, another chapter of our lives. Since I was still teaching, George finishing first grade, we would relocate sometime over the summer, as soon as our house sold. Putting the house on the market meant completing the renovations we'd been putting off—new linoleum in the kitchen, repairing cement on the back step—and decluttering cupboards, drawers, and closets. Blake stayed with his dad in Bryant during the week and joined us in Dell Rapids on Friday nights.

One Friday after school, while I waited for Blake to arrive, I stood in the bathroom, throwing out expired children's Tylenol, tubes of hotel shampoo, and half empty bottles of scented lotion, packing useful toiletries between towels and rolls of toilet paper in a large tote. The garbage can was already overflowing when I moved up to the second shelf, where I found at least a dozen orange prescription bottles, all labeled "Jensen, Blake." Most contained only chalky remains of the pills that once rattled in them, others still clamored with pink or white capsules. Each bottle that I flipped into the trash was a reminder of the pain and addiction Blake had fought his way through. But then a bottle rattled. Unfamiliar blue pills. I read the label: morphine.

My first reaction was panic. Get it out of my house. A quick Google search confirmed, morphine was flushable. Once the pills were gone, I could breathe. I sat on the bathroom counter thinking about the questions I hadn't asked, the truths Blake hadn't revealed. I didn't think he had filled the prescription. I probably should've known—Blake's way of disagreeing had always been to pretend that he might agree—or at least asked. Now, the information hung in the air as I packed. Maybe I should have counted the pills before I flushed them. Had he been taking them this whole time?

When Blake arrived, the question fluttered in my stomach as I watched him hug the kids. At supper, I studied his laughter, the movements of his hands. I offered him a beer, and when he waved it off—"Maybe later"—I studied his answer, wondering if he spent weeknights drinking with his dad, and searched his face for signs—of what, I didn't know. When the kids were finally in bed, Blake and I sat in the living room, dimly lit by the TV, walls bare, boxes stacked against them. I slid forward in the recliner, inching closer to Blake, who sat on the couch, and said, finally, "I sorted through all your old prescriptions today. I found the morphine." Blake nodded, unsurprised. "I didn't think you filled that prescription."

I watched his face as he answered without hesitating, "Oh yeah, I filled it."

"Did you take it?"

"Up until the surgery, yeah." He looked me in the eye. "It didn't help at all. I even took it with the hydrocodone. That didn't do anything, either."

I sat for a moment in the fog of this truth: Blake had mixed hydrocodone and morphine. In our house. While caring for our kids. While driving to work. Yes, he'd been addicted to pain medicine, but that was unintentional, unknowing. I'd asked him not to take the morphine. He had knowingly mixed drugs that shouldn't be mixed. Blake downplayed it all. "It was just for those two weeks. I guess when you're desperate to feel better, you'll do just about anything."

There it was again. Desperation. If Blake had been desperate enough to mix prescription pain medicine, what else might he have done? What other dangers had we brushed up against? How close had we come to a different ending to our story? What dangers lay before us now? Our past and our future—what I thought I knew— felt suddenly blurred. The air in our living room grew dense. I felt myself swallowed, again, by fog, sensing, again, the possibility of a dangerous plummet. Blake had hovered at the mouth of the abyss of addiction, unknowingly dependent, desperate for relief. I had observed it all, seen none of it. He had experienced it all, named none of it. What else was I missing? What might bring him back to the edge of that abyss? Tears collected as I realized that seven years after Blake's safe return from war, I still felt on the verge of losing him.

Nine

WE WERE ON THE VERGE OF SO MANY THINGS, and life felt on the verge of blossoming, too, into something more beautiful than it had previously been. As we waited for our house in Dell Rapids to sell, we hunted for our next home in De Smet. Once school was out, George, Addie, and I joined Blake in Bryant, where we all lived out of a suitcase at my parents' house. While Blake worked, I house hunted via internet, usually finding the same handful of results: a couple houses beyond our budget, several plots of land, a couple houses that were too small or needed too much work. My mom and I drove the streets, calling numbers on For Sale signs we spotted in yards. More of the same. We toured one house in the right price range and in the right "quadrant" of town, as Blake liked to call it, where the kids could walk to school without crossing either of the state highways that intersected town. It had the three bedrooms we needed but was cramped with absolutely no yard. "It would work," I told Blake, when I called him afterwards. "But it would feel so tight. It just didn't feel like home." As I drove down the street with tears in my eyes, I spotted a brick two-story with white trim, a big yard, and a small front porch framed by white pillars. I whined, "Why can't that house be for sale?"

"We'll just keep looking," Blake said calmly. "We're not in any hurry here. Our house in Dell Rapids hasn't sold yet, anyway. And we can stay with my dad or with your parents as long as we need to."

It was true. While we searched for houses, the kids and I spent out summer in limbo, time divided between my parents' house in Bryant and our home in Dell Rapids. I decided to plant a garden, spontaneous and small. A metaphorical planting of roots. An attempt to feel established. The garden was out of town, beside the barn where Blake's family raised pheasants, so we had water supply and room for anything I could imagine growing. I kept it simple. I let George and Addie plant peppers, tomatoes, and cucumbers while I sprinkled finer seeds in haphazard rows and poked beans into the ground. The kids ended up caked in mud from head to toe, and I had to redo some of their planting, but the garden became a place for the kids and I to escape. They could play outside, I could weed and water, and the resilient roots took hold, plants producing enough for me to can a few pickles and stewed tomatoes.

Still, the live-in situation was getting stressful. My parents had moved, so now instead of an upstairs bedroom with a separate living room, bathroom, and entry to the house, we inhabited a basement. Still with a separate bathroom and a living room, but now, with kids on the verge of eight and four, it was harder to contain noise and messes. Then our two-year-old house cat, Runner, started fighting with my mom's cat, Ford, through the window at night. They would yowl, hiss, and scratch at the window screen. It was ridiculous. Then, one day Ford spotted Runner through the open garage door. Sensing opportunity, Ford attacked. The cats rolled down the stairs in a tangled mess of orange and black. My mom cheered, "Get her, Ford!" I sensed the tension wasn't just between our cats. It was time for us to go.

There were other signs, too. One night, I woke up and realized Blake wasn't in the bed beside me. I couldn't remember with any certainty whether he'd been there. Did he leave in the middle of the night? Or did he not come home? I checked the bathroom, the living room couch. Nothing. I went outside to check for his car. It wasn't in the driveway. I called his phone. No answer. But that wasn't surprising. Blake was notoriously bad at answering his phone, and if he was out somewhere and thought I was mad, he was probably less likely to answer than ever. I ran through rational explanations: he drank too much and stayed at his dad's, or maybe he was upset about something and stayed at his dad's. Without stopping to think, I dialed my father-in-law. It was 3 a.m., but he answered. He sounded concerned. "No, Amber, I don't think he's here. He was, and he stayed pretty late, but I'm sure he left quite a while ago." *What the fuck?* I wondered. *Where is he? Did he stagger off somewhere?*

I went outside and paced in the cool, dark, summer. What if he drove somewhere? What if he had an accident? I couldn't shake the feeling that something was wrong. I went back inside and paced the living room, and that's when I heard the rustle of sheets from the second downstairs bedroom. I opened the door to find Blake there, asleep, in a bed and a room we'd never slept in before. My frustration let loose. I shook him awake. "What the hell are you doing?" I whispered.

He responded so quickly, I doubted he'd even been sleeping. "I don't know," he said.

"You don't know? You scared me. I thought you were dead."

He didn't make excuses. "I'm sorry. I don't know what's going on with me."

His sincerity softened my anger. "You can't just do this, Blake. You can't hide from me. What is going on?"

I knew what it was like to not want to ask for help, so when he said, "I really don't know. I mean, I know life isn't as bad as it feels like it is. We're fine. We'll be fine. But, I just feel like, I think I need help."

I leaned down to lay my head on his bare chest. "We can get help." I listened to the muffled metronome of Blake's heart. I breathed purposefully in time with the rhythms of his body. "But don't scare me like this, please. Just come to bed." I sat up, slid my hand to his shoulder, and tugged, but he lay still.

"I think I should just sleep here. I promise I'm fine. But I just need to stay here."

Exhausted and relieved, I whispered, "You're sure you're OK?"

"I will be," he promised.

"We'll talk in the morning," I said. The dim light from an egress window side-lit his nod. "You promise?"

He nodded again and whispered, "Thanks."

I sighed, and lay my head against his chest again, for just a moment, before I went back to the bed on the other side of the wall, where I lay, willing him to feel my presence through the layers of sheetrock that separated us. *I'm right here*, I thought. *Don't push me away*. My thoughts were a prayer, a reaching, an extension of myself toward him, and extension of ourselves toward something bigger than us, something that could guide us.

In the morning, we did talk, and he agreed to go see our old family doctor in Sioux Falls. While he was gone, I researched long-term effects of opioid addiction, depression among them. The drug worked by inhibiting receptors in the brain—numbing them or depressing them—and those depressive effects could last years. A lifetime. This was another instance of pain ignored. Pain swelling to exquisite tenderness, demanding attention.

Blake wouldn't let me go with him to the doctor, but when he returned, he said he had a plan. Something to get him through a few months, then he would see how things were going. Dr. Boyens didn't think it had to be long term. I thanked him for going, for being willing to have that conversation, take that medicine, because I knew he hated it. And I insisted, "I really think we need to find our own place, Blake. I don't think living the way we're living helps." We agreed. We teetered on the edge of the abyss, yet again, but held each other steady.

WHEN OUR HOUSE IN DELL RAPIDS FINALLY SOLD, the urgency of our house hunt increased. I obsessively checked internet listings, one in particular that I liked, even though the price was higher than we wished. Then, one day my internet search produced a picture of a red brick house with white trim. I called Blake. "You remember that house I wished was for sale? The brick house with the yard? Well, it is." I called the realtor to set up a showing.

"You're right," Blake said, as we waited outside the house. "This is a cool house." We could see his office building, kitty corner across the highway, from the front yard. When the realtor led us in the front door to the living room, we were greeted by original built-ins, wood floors, and wide baseboards. When I turned to Blake, he was smiling.

When we were first married, Blake and I went to open houses for fun—we enjoyed dreaming about our preferred layouts and finishes. Searching for our home in Dell Rapids was a bit more strained because we were anxious to move, but George had enjoyed the process, commenting on floors, and countertops, and paint colors as we assessed each one. House hunting in De Smet was stressful due to low inventory and urgency. But of all the houses we'd toured in all those places, this depression-era two story with a large lot, a two-stall garage, three bedrooms, and a ton of character was the first that screamed *home*. Blake even noticed the glass doorknobs. It was the first time I'd seen him have an emotional reaction to a house, and we couldn't wait to make an offer.

We didn't paint. We didn't refinish the floors. We just moved in as soon as we could, which turned out to be a week after the kids started at their new school—Addie in her first year of pre-K, George in second grade—and just in time to celebrate both of their October birthdays. George settled in quickly to his class of seventeen students, and he liked his teacher, Mrs. Somsen. He sounded excited when he told me that the elementary chorus would sing at the community Veterans Day program, which was uncharacteristic of the boy whose lips barely moved when the Sunday School kids sang in church. "I told my teacher that my dad and my uncles are veterans," he said, his eyebrows arching. "Do you think they'll be there?"

Careful with my words, I answered, "We'll have to ask them about their plans."

Since returning from Iraq, Blake's Veterans Day tradition had included taking the day off from work and hunting with his brothers and dad. Even when we lived almost a hundred miles from Bryant, Blake had made the drive and had often spent a night or two there for his Veterans Day hunting trip. But, I reasoned, now that home and hunting ground were only twenty miles from George's school, maybe he could come to the program. Actually, I knew he *could* come. I just hoped that he would. So that night, I asked him. He answered, "I'm sure we could make that work."

I nodded in relief, accepting the answer as the one I wanted to hear, assuming Blake was planning to come, forgetting that he would avoid telling me if he wasn't. Eight and a half years of marriage should have taught me to read his response more accurately, but it didn't. So, on the day of the program, as I prepared George for school and reminded Blake of the 10:00 a.m. program, I was surprised when he said, "If we aren't in the middle of a hunt, I'm sure we can come over."

I felt sick. I looked up from tying George's shoes to meet his wide brown eyes. He knew as well as I did. Wanting to defend George, deflect his disappointment, I demanded clarification. As Blake made his way toward the door. I looked at the floor and asked, "You're not going to come, are you?"

Blake answered matter-of-factly, "Probably not. But I'll come get George later if he wants to spend the day with us. George has earned Veterans Day as much as anyone."

I jumped up and followed Blake to the back porch. As he slipped on his boots, I fumbled noisily through baskets, searching out a pair of thin gloves and a hat for George. I didn't know what to say but needed to say something. I wished I could change Blake's mind. I stared into the mountain of mismatched gloves, tears collecting in my eyes as Blake gave a final tug on his boot laces and stood. I pinched my eyes shut, bracing myself for the sound of the door, but Blake paused. "So, you'll just call me when the program's over, then?" His tone was even, guiltless.

I lifted my eyes and turned, not toward Blake, but toward the window. Determined to make him acknowledge his choice, I hissed, "You could come back for the program. It would mean a lot to him."

Without a word, the door opened and shut. Blake didn't reach back to lock the screen door into place, so it flapped in the wind. I cried and watched him walk over dead grass and past leafless trees then disappear into the garage. Then, picturing George, his ears perked, eyebrows raised, back in the living room, I forced anger out in a slow, audible exhale.

When I re-entered the living room, George's eyes followed me. When I sat beside him, he dropped his gaze to the floor. I wasn't sure how to handle the severing of the connection George had wanted to build. My son whispered his understanding. "He's not coming?"

"No," I said. I put my arm around him and pulled him into my side. "But he'll come back later to pick you up, if you want to spend the rest of the day with him."

"So, I won't have school in the afternoon?"

"No. I'll talk to your teacher. You can just come home with me from the program, does that sound good?"

"I guess." George shrugged, his words almost invisible, like traces of erased pencil lead.

"Your dad said you deserve to celebrate Veterans Day as much as anyone. Do you know what he meant?" George shook his head yes, but his down-turned eyes read no. "He meant that you spent a year without a dad. That you deserve to spend every Veterans Day with him." I created my own understanding as I explained. "And I think he meant that he missed the first year of your life, so he wants to spend every Veterans Day with you, too, but not with all those other people."

At the program later that morning, with Addie squirming on my lap, I watched veterans from all branches of the military stand for recognition as their names were called, one by one, in a touching tribute. I couldn't see George, since the elementary chorus was seated in the bleachers directly to my right, but I imagined his serious expression, staring straight forward, pretending not to notice that his dad wasn't there. I wondered if his eyes burned like mine. Part of me wanted to believe that Blake had snuck in, that we would hear his name and see him pop up from the crowd in the bleachers across from us, but I knew better. In fact, I laughed knowing that if Blake had snuck in, they would never call his name, because he wouldn't have filled out the slip of paper at the doorway asking for his name, military branch, and years of service. I leaned my temple against Addie's head and closed my eyes, picturing Blake in the passenger seat of the farm truck, or trudging through a field, or perched in a tree, waiting out a trophy deer. I imagined him squinting in concentration as he studied the tree line, listened for leaves crunching, branches snapping, and I understood why Blake wouldn't be happy there in that packed auditorium. He didn't want to hear his name or listen to the band's medley of military marches. I realized that he would not be taking orders from anyone on Veterans Day. Instead, he would breathe deep, feel the autumn breeze on his cheeks, hear leaves crunch beneath his feet. On Veterans Day, he would enjoy the fruits of his summer labor of planting and weeding, spraying and staking. On Veterans Day, he would take shelter among the trees.

IN ANOTHER YEAR, I tried to do better, tried to get it right. I asked that George be excused from singing in his third grade Veterans Day program, explaining to his teacher that he and his dad would be spending the day together. "It's kind of a tradition," I apologized. She had no reservations.

Blake's hunting day began before sunrise, so the kids and I slept in and spent the morning making soup for the hunters. We met them at my father-in-law's, where we ate out of paper bowls in the shed, surrounded by dozens of mounted deer, antelope antlers, and assorted waterfowl. The shed acted as a sort of hunting lodge and private taxidermy museum I'd grown so accustomed to that I could forget I used to feel uneasy in the presence of all those bones and dead eyes. I'd adapted to the environment, but Blake was native to it. This was his comfort zone. The two-story white house next to the shed housed the small table—pushed up against the wall until mealtime, then pulled out to the middle of the kitchen floor for more seating—where the Jensen family ate venison and cheese whiz mac and cheese. Its closets contained boxes of old photos, totes full of hunting gear.

Blake's demeanor in the shed reminded me of his dugout persona. He leaned back into his chair, told stories about Brandy, the best hunting dog they'd ever had, jumping off a house after a coon and their dad sending them into culverts with flashlights to scare out prey. He was confident, calm, laughed easily. As he began to pull on layers—jeans over the long johns he'd stripped down to for lunch, an extra quarter-zip fleece—before tucking everything into overalls and lacing boots that looked like they weighed ten pounds each, Blake shed the layers of anxiety and reserve he wore in so many other situations. Watching this shedding reassured me that this was where he needed to be on Veterans Day, even if it meant that spending it together meant only a few hours for lunch. This was the heart of him, and being in touch with something even more central to his identity than his military experience seemed like an appropriate way to spend a day that would inevitably lead to some difficult memories, some soul searching.

"It gets dark pretty early," Blake explained as he pulled on his gloves and hat. "We've gotta get in the stands before the deer start moving."

I nodded my understanding, but I wished I could explain to Blake that I wasn't mad anymore, and that I understood how he needed this day. Instead, I just said, "Of course. Was there anything else you wanted to do? With George? Or should we just go home?"

Blake turned to George. "Do you wanna drive around for a little bit? Check things out?"

George shrugged. He looked up at me.

"It's up to you. You sure can," I encouraged.

He shrugged again.

"It's OK if you don't want to," Blake said. "When you get a little older you can sit with us. In a few years, you'll be able to get your own deer tag."

George leaned into my hip. I tousled his mousy hair. "Does that sound good? Should we just meet him back at home later?" He nodded shyly. "OK, I'll grab Addie." I lifted her from the recliner where she had fallen asleep, snuggling with the current best hunting dog, Millie. Part of me wished Blake would insist a little more, take George out for just a little bit, to establish this new tradition. But most of me relaxed into the uncertainty. We would figure it out. All of it. All of our story. Because I was finally beginning to understand how deeply conflicted my veteran husband was, how close I had come—how close I still was—to losing him to that war that he fought in and survived, and how tragically common this story is. Ours was the story of a veteran of war who came home with no visible injuries, no PTSD—a veteran who gets by financially and whose family holds together. Ours seemed like an easy, happy ending. Ours was an invisibly normal story.

But the invisible parts of our story were filled with tragic possibilities and inevitable struggles. I had listened to Blake chuckle—the deep, rumbling laugh that ricocheted in his chest when the only alternative to laughter is the desperate cry of a cornered animal—when he admitted that during his VA treatment, while still in the clutches of chronic pain, he couldn't imagine life continuing. That when he considered taking out a life insurance policy, it was because knew he was going to die. I had heard Blake admit that addiction still pulsed through his veins, and, sometimes, his body still longed for the pain meds prescribed to him for so many years. And I'd felt Blake's body stiffen at the touch of my hand, recognized this as a sign that depression had once again swept over him. I watched Blake and his son connect easily, but still remain distant, and I had known somewhere inside that things wouldn't have been this way—not this way exactly—if Blake hadn't missed the first year of George's life. And I was beginning to understand how unique our story was and at once how common. Not singular, but plural—the story of many veterans. Not singular, but multiple—one of many possible versions. Not singular, but collective—reflecting the experience of past generations, reverberating into the future.

One day the following spring, as Addie and I walked from our house to the park in De Smet, we passed the high school, attached by a gymnasium to the National Guard Armory. A truck was pulled up to the step on the south side of the building, and men in uniform laughed as they loaded it with equipment. Addie took my hand. She looked up at me with her blue eyes as she asked, "Who are those guys?"

"Soldiers," I answered. I'd never seen any actual Army activity at the armory as long as we'd lived in town, and I knew that if she had more questions about what they were doing, I wouldn't have any answers. I was as surprised to see them as she was. But she seemed satisfied with my answer.

An hour later, when we walked back by the armory, which was quiet now, Addie slowed near the steps where we'd seen the truck. "Mom," she said, looking up at me with a face that struck me, suddenly, as very grown up. "Is my dad a soldier?" The care she took with her words brought tears to my eyes.

"Yes, sweet pea." I smiled down at her. "He was a soldier. But I guess now you would call him a veteran." It hit me that since Blake was out of the National Guard before she was born, she'd never seen him in uniform. She seemed to be thinking hard, trying to piece it all together, and I was struck by how difficult that might be. I invited her to explore whatever questions she might have, asking, "Do you know what that means?"

She nodded, slipping her tiny hand into mine, asking innocently, "Did my dad go to war?"

A big question for such a little girl. "Yes, he did. He was in the war in Iraq. Have you heard of that?"

She nodded again, then asked, without hesitation, as if she'd thought about this before. "What did he do there?"

"He trained Iraqi police," I said. "He tried to teach them how to take care of their country, how to keep people safe."

The answer satisfied her. "So, he was a good guy."

"Yes, your dad was a good guy." I wanted to sweep her up in my arms and protect her from these questions. "Your dad *is* a good guy."

She giggled, "Yeah." Then her laugh trailed off and her face settled into a squinting seriousness. "I don't know why, but on Veterans Day, I always feel kind of," she searched for the right word and settled on one, "proud."

My breath escaped audibly, as if my chest had collapsed, her sincerity crushing me. I stopped to kneel down and look her in the eye. "That's a good feeling. And you're right. You should feel proud." I hugged her, noticing, like I did when she crawled in to bed beside me at night, how small she still was. I hugged her firmly, but gently, as if I didn't want to crush her.

I wanted to spill it all out, right there, explain that her dad had served with all the right intentions. How he really had wanted to help. But how maybe it wasn't that easy. How being a soldier, a veteran, was hard, sometimes. And that some of the times when he was quiet or sad, when he came home from work and didn't want to play, that some of that was part of being a soldier too. I pictured sunny evenings, the kids begging Blake to play soccer with them after supper, his harsh reply. "Not now, kiddo. I need to let my food settle." How we all knew that meant he didn't feel like playing. That he probably would stay glued to the couch, eventually reclining back and closing his eyes while the TV droned on. I pictured George—the way those words crushed him, the way he retreated to his room and his Legos, or outside alone, the way I rushed to connect with him, knowing what he longed for. And then I pictured Addie, her response so different to those same events. Addie didn't give up on her dad when he was depressed or tired. She changed her approach. She gathered coloring books and papers, a box of markers, and slipped on to the couch near her dad. At first, she would color quietly, at a safe distance, then slowly inch toward him. Eventually she might ask him, "What color is Peppa Pig's dress, Dad? What color should I use?" If Blake answered, she might select the red he suggested, then ask, "Her boots? What color are they?" Grabbing the yellow he pointed to, she might snuggle closer and ask. "Can you help me color them?" After her questions about Blake's military service, I couldn't help but read her interactions a bit differently. She was intuitive. In touch with her dad. And fearless. Finding a way to connect with him.

Ever since we learned that Blake would be deployed to Iraq, I'd been considering how that deployment would affect our family, but I'd thought most about Blake and George, to a lesser extent me, and least of all, Addie. But the military was undoubtedly a part of each of our stories, a part of our family story, still unfolding. Blake was tagged with the identity of soldier by cultural narrative, family history, and personal choice. Once he joined the military, he carried physical tags—oblong metal plates, stamped with his name, social security number, blood type, and maybe his religious preference—but the label became integral to his identity, meaning multiplying through experience. The kids and I didn't wear physical tags. We didn't experience military life directly. In fact, we heard very little about it. But it was still a part of us.

I'd asked Blake about his dog tags, once, and he said he wasn't sure where they were. I'd read that soldiers during Vietnam began the practice of wearing rubber silencers around their dog tags so they wouldn't chime when they walked, giving away their position. I imagined Blake's tucked in one of the black boxes at the bottom of his dad's basement stairs, the ones he shipped home from Iraq full of Kurt Vonnegut books and letters from home. And I imagined George and Addie discovering them someday. I didn't want the dog tags to be a surprise, the stories associated with them a secret, but it's so easy to silence ourselves, especially when stories are sad or complicated. Especially in the military. Especially in the Midwest, in our family, where we avoid confrontation and internalize the most conflicted stories, fearing that, like noisy dog tags, they might make us vulnerable. I remembered the image of my Grandpa Dayton in his uniform, the limited stories I heard about him, and the limitless tragedy of his dying young, how all that shaped me. The silence sparked my interest in literature and movies about war. The stories became the lens through which I viewed my own experience as a military wife, the possibility of tragedy in our lives. These stories—told and untold—were part of us. We were tagged, as if in a game where we were all it, collecting memories, chasing meaning.

As Addie, whose curls collected around her face in the humidity, asked me for the first time about her dad's military service, I felt the relief that comes with storytelling. The potential for connection and understanding. Because there is danger in silence, in not naming the challenges we face, in not sharing our burdens and asking our questions. When we find words, we can create the possibility of recovery, renewal, and growth.

THAT SPRING, AS WE PREPARED for another year of gardening,

another season of growth, Blake expressed interest in the garden. He'd always enjoyed the outdoors, but it had never occurred to me that he would enjoy gardening. He thought we should add potatoes and onions, carrots and peas, and more of everything. If the garden was expanding, I thought it should include Swiss chard and zucchini. That year, as the scope of our garden grew, I froze green beans, canned salsa, and spaghetti sauce. Gardening became more of a commitment than a hobby.

The time wasn't a problem for Blake. After almost twenty years of amateur baseball, after his back surgery, and just as he started to feel good enough to play again, the Bryant Bucs amateur team had folded. He'd tried to keep it alive, but each game day consisted of phone calls, begging players to come just to get nine guys on the field. There was added responsibility: dragging the infield, keeping grass free of weeds, chalking lines, packing the pitcher's mound. After years of chronic pain had pulled him from the game, he felt, in his words, like a kid again and looked like one, too, comfortably scooping balls from the dirt at first and confidently running the bases, but he couldn't keep it going. The team dissolved. So, Blake busied himself with mowing—his dad's yard, his grandma's yard, and Marilyn Anderson's—and tending to the pheasant chores. Gardening was a welcome addition.

Gardening legitimized Blake's habit of driving the seventeen miles from De Smet to Bryant every day after work. He fed and watered the pheasants, but also weeded and watered the garden, which made me resent the fact that he spent every evening away from home just a little less. Blake was proud of the garden, and it gave us a common hobby. Now, instead of watching him play baseball twice a week, when we were in Bryant, he would ask, "Should we take a garden tour?" The tour always involved a walk between rows, the plucking of a few cucumbers, maybe the trimming of herbs, and plans for expanding the garden further the next year, maybe adding ornamental corn or a new variety of beans, but always more pumpkins. Blake had become obsessed with pumpkins—miniature pumpkins, bumpy, gourd-like pumpkins, white pumpkins, and giant pumpkins. I rolled my eyes at the giant pumpkins, reminding Blake that they served absolutely no purpose, but I knew there was an unofficial pumpkin-growing competition in the Jensen family, started by Blake's Grandpa Bob, who loved rolling a giant pumpkin to the end of the driveway—a display for anyone passing by on South Dakota Highway 25. So, I relented. "Grow as many pumpkins as you like."

The garden tour usually ended with a beer or two, sipped in the shade of the barn, which is probably why Blake came to consider these tours dates. I wasn't sure dates should involve that much bug spray or require the scrubbing of dirt out of fingernails, but George and Addie avoided the garden unless they were allowed to free range with the hose and shovels, so it was usually just the two of us. Our form of romance.

By the next summer, Blake had spent the winter planning. We would double the size of the garden and add a plot behind the barn. He drew a map, planning the spacing between rows. He scoured catalogs for new and interesting seeds. "Have you ever dried beans? Like kidney beans?" he asked. No, I hadn't, but if he wanted to try, we should go for it. He rounded up stakes and tied a string between them to mark out straight, even rows. He pounded fence posts into the ground and wired cow panels in between as pea trellises. The garden date ritual evolved into a regular Friday night event, with Blake adding ice to a cooler full of Coors Light early in the evening in preparation. After weeding, picking, and planning, we each grabbed a beer and a lawn chair. We reminisced about the early years of our friendship, the relationship that developed in the dugout of the Bryant baseball field, the tree wrangling and our honeymoon road trip across the state in a pickup with no air conditioning, and about the five homes we'd lived in in our ten years together. We retold baseball stories—my cousin Rob's called home run, Blake's homerun in his first amateur at bat, and Steve Pietila's painted on pinstripe pants. The barn became our new dugout, a sheltered space for connection, and our relationship grew along with the garden. It wasn't the visible progress of young plants that double in size in weeks' time, but the slow growth of trees, notable and measurable in the long term, each year of our marriage a tree ring—some wide, evidence of good weather and optimal growth, others thin and light, documenting a good spring but harsh winter—layers of growth documented over years and decades, and more steady than it seems.

As we settled into our home in De Smet, we settled into a sense of community and connection. George and Addie thrived in the small school, with classes of less than twenty students, circles of close friends. George gained confidence as a basketball player. Addie discovered a love for gymnastics. I played preludes, liturgy, and hymns most Sundays at Our Redeemer Church, where Blake and I had attended Sunday School and confirmation, where we were married, where our kids were baptized. Blake got involved in church council, becoming a deacon, which meant the kids helped him serve communion the first and fourth Sundays of each month. Blake began attending American Legion meetings with Bryant's Post 37. He'd been a paying member since he joined the Army at age eighteen, but as an active member, he helped serve the annual pancake breakfast, present the colors at funerals and sporting events, and emceed the annual Memorial Day program. Blake even found a home on a new baseball team.

Since moving from Legion to amateur baseball, Blake had

played every game in a Kelly-green Bryant Bucs jersey. For years his beer of choice was Old Mil Light, because that's what the Bryant Bucs drank in the dugout after games. So, when the coach of Bryant's rival, the Lake Norden Lakers, learned that Blake might still be interested in playing and asked Blake to join their team, he hesitated. I encouraged him. Burt, the Lakers coach, was a family friend—he grew up just down the road from my dad, and I often heard them say the kids of the two families felt more like siblings than friends—but even more, Burt was a baseball guy. Even if they'd spent their careers cheering against each other, I knew they both relished the pristine beauty of a freshly raked field, the satisfaction of a well-placed line drive.

"Burt would love to have you," I assured him. "And I know you'd love to play again."

"But the Lakers, Amber?" Blake shook his head. "Too much history."

There was a lot of history. Decades of Fourth of July match ups that Bryant never won. My cousin's husband hitting a home run so far that when he crossed home plate, Burt was there to meet him, asking the umpire to check his bat. There was also the time Blake was ejected, mixing up the insult he yelled at the ump after a called third strike, spitting out *You've got bats like an ear!* instead of ears like a bat. But after sitting on the invitation for two weeks, Blake finally relented, and texted Burt to say he'd give it a try.

Blake came home from the first practice, grinning. "It was great. Burt runs a great practice—we actually did drills and stuff—and it's just nice to be around baseball guys."

The feeling was mutual. At the first game that season, Burt's wife, Linda, who had taught both Blake and I in kindergarten, approached me. "Amber, it's so good to see you here," she beamed. "And I just have to tell you how much Burt enjoys having Blake on the team. He says, 'You know, some of us just have baseball in our blood. Blake is one of us.'"

I assured Linda that Blake felt the same way and asked her to thank Burt for giving baseball back to Blake. I gave her the shortened version of Blake's struggles with chronic pain, his experience with the VA. Tears collected in her eyes as she said, sincerely, "It's really great to have him on the team. To see you and the kids. That's what it's all about."

She was right. Baseball was a family affair. George assumed the role of batboy, and Burt gave him a Lakers T-shirt and a cap to legitimize him as part of the team. At the first game of the season, I reconnected with my friend, Kristi, whose husband was the most talented player on the team—still pitching shut outs and catching entire games well into his forties—and a former team-mate of Blake's in Bryant. He'd made the shift from Bucs green to Lakers blue. Blake could do it too. Kristi babysat the Jensen brothers when they were kids, and she'd witnessed the early years of Blake and I flirting and known I was in love with Blake way back when he got kicked out of that Lakers game. And she was there when he snuck back in and hid between Kristi and I on our blanket, accepting the beer we offered him, and laughing at the absurdity of his ejection. We were baseball wives, and our children were baseball kids. Our daughters instantly became friends. As the team trotted out to warm up near the outfield fence, I followed Blake's distinct, stiff-armed run, which made him stand out, even in a crowd of matching pinstripes. I relished his broad smile as he coaxed a younger player into a game, tipping the ball back and forth with thick barreled bats, diving to keep it from touching the ground. Others joined, and soon six or seven grown men circled, lunging for saves, cheering to keep the streak going, collectively sighing when the ball fell to the grass.

When the game started with the Lakers the away team, I didn't have to wait long to see my favorite part of the game: Blake at bat. A navy-blue helmet shaded his face, but I could picture him, squinting in concentration. I admired his upright stance—not the squatted intensity of many players, but tall and steady, weight shifting like a tree swaying just slightly in the wind, not pushed by the elements, but in harmony with them. I joked to Kristi, "Watch him take a walk here." She laughed, as I added, "No one gets walked as much as Blake." As he stepped into the batter's box, we both knew he wouldn't swing at the first pitch. He wouldn't swing until he was sure he could connect.

Ten

ANOTHER SPRING BROUGHT ANOTHER GARDEN—still bigger than the last. As Memorial Day approached, Blake and I prepared to celebrate twelve years of marriage. Blake would emcee the Legion's Community Memorial Day program, as had become the norm. He wrote out and practiced his script, like he did every year, but planned a special thank you for my sister, my niece Cami, and I. We would provide special music, at the request of the American Legion Auxiliary ladies, and Blake threatened to comment, "God bless them, they try," as we exited the stage. On the day of the program, at the podium in a blue Legion jacket and VFW hat, Blake didn't have the heart to deliver his joke, but in keeping with tradition, he mispronounced the names of the Hemr kids who read "Flanders Fields" and "America's Answer" each year. He followed his script, asking the audience to stand at the appropriate times, introducing the chaplain, commander, and finally that year's guest speaker, who voiced concern that, as a country, we were becoming detached from the sacrifice of military service in what was becoming known as the Forever War.

When the speaker explained his intention—to read the names of the twenty-six South Dakota soldiers killed in the ongoing conflicts in Iraq and Afghanistan—my body stiffened as I prepared myself for a list of names, at least four of which I knew I would recognize. I focused on Blake, whose comfortable demeanor shifted as the wave of familiar names came. Richard Schild and Daniel Cuka, December 2005. Allen Kokesh, February 2006. Gregory Wagner, May 2006. Blake's gaze dropped to the floor. I detected his hands, fingers spread wide, moving almost imperceptibly, tapping his thighs. Tears filled my eyes at the thought of these soldiers, their families, and at the sight of my husband, bracing himself against the memory. A question I'd always intended but never remembered to ask surfaced. I knew it was Greg's name that impacted Blake most. Blake had described Greg's death as the sucker punch, the one that caught him off guard, took the air out of him, and as I watched him on stage, confronting that pain, I felt a sudden need to understand.

On our next garden date, after we'd toured and weeded and sat in our lawn chairs with our beers, the conversation started lightly. "I was thinking, next year, we really need better tomato cages," Blake said. "These crappy ones get all twisted up and break."

I nodded. "But the big sturdy ones are expensive. Maybe we should make them. My mom always did." We weighed the options—building cages ourselves from wooden frames or heavy wire cattle panels, or buying expensive, heavy-duty cages from the farm supply store—and vowed to figure it out next year.

Our conversation meandered from gardening to the upcoming week's schedule. We ran through our usual discussion of the kids, parenting challenges, and finally future plans. I asked, "Do you think we've outgrown our house?" I answered my own question. "I think it's starting to feel cramped. Like we need space for the kids to play, to hang out with their friends."

Blake shrugged as he popped a beer tab. "I don't know. It's not that bad, is it?"

"Not in the summer, when the kids spend most of their time outside," I agreed. "But you can get awfully cranky in the winter when the kids are playing in the living room while you're trying to watch TV."

"They can play in the basement," Blake said. "We always tell them, go play in the basement if you want to be wild."

"Yeah, but the basement's not that nice." I'd painted the cement floors and cinderblock walls. It was a good place for bouncing balls and messy craft projects but not much else. "Do you really think they want to hang out with friends down there?"

"Maybe not," Blake agreed, "but I always thought that if we moved, we'd move to an acreage. Like Marilyn's. So, I think we have to hold out for that."

I knew he dreamed of Marilyn Anderson's, with its rows of trees and pastures, meticulous barns, a perfect spot right along the highway, just over a mile from where we sat, overlooking our garden. Blake and his cousins had been mowing her yard for years, since Dean passed away, so he'd had plenty of time to dream. The question was whether we'd be ready to buy when Marilyn was ready to sell. Her children had convinced her to move to the east coast, to live closer to them, but they hadn't convinced her to sell the farm, yet. Blake was patient, as always, but I felt an urgency. "If we were going to live on an acreage, I'd want it to be now," I said. "While the kids could enjoy it. Addie could have her chickens. George could show rabbits in 4H or something. I just wish they were ready to sell."

"But financially, the longer we wait, the better," Blake said. I understood the logic, but I knew he'd want to take the chance whenever it presented itself. He confirmed my suspicion, saying, "It would be nice to plant some apple trees." Then he raised an eyebrow at me and added, "We could even have more kids." He laughed the loud, sinister laugh that shows he's really pleased with an idea, really feels he's clever. "And *they* could enjoy the farm." I rolled my eyes. "You know I'm serious," Blake added. "I'd have a dozen kids if you wanted to, but you do most of the work in that department, so I know it's not really up to me."

The comment stung a little bit, even though I appreciated on some level that he at least acknowledged the imbalance in our domestic duties. I still resented sometimes how much Blake's time was just that—his time—while mine seemed always occupied. If I wanted to go for a run or have a drink with friends, I scheduled it around or during Addie's gymnastics practice, George's baseball or basketball, and my own work demands. When Blake came home from work, he assumed that he could run to the pheasant farm or go hunting, unless I told him differently. But I did understand that Blake was happiest, healthiest, when he was outdoors, hunting, among trees, or with his hands in the dirt. I understood this even before I researched the therapeutic benefits of nature, but information convinced me that fresh air was Blake's mood stabilizing drug, and it was better than most of the alternatives. That didn't mean it didn't complicate my life sometimes. It did mean that I couldn't imagine having a third child.

I deflected Blake's casual invitation to have more kids, twisting one side of my mouth in a disapproving smile. "Yeah, I don't think so," I said. "But I'll be sure to let you know if I change my mind. I mean, I have to admit, when I see those pictures of baby George . . . "

Blake finished the thought, "With his perfectly round head, hands as big as baseball mitts."

I smiled and added, "And Addie, with those ridiculously chubby cheeks, those curls around her ears, her little hands cradling a baby doll."

Blake inhaled a deep, quiet laugh and said, "You know, I hardly remember those years." I looked at him, puzzled. "I mean when Addie was a baby. When we lived in Dell Rapids."

I thought this was another joke, like his story of traveling halfway around the world to avoid the delivery room, but he ruled out that possibility. "I mean, George," he said. "I remember George. He was an easy baby. Never cried, never spit up on me. Perfect angel. Addie...I don't remember. I feel awful about that."

I blinked, examining this revelation. "You mean you don't remember the stories," I said. "Like her smashing George's Lego Clone Turbo Tank."

"No, I mean pretty much all of it," Blake clarified. "All of those years, not just Addie. I mean I remember the house, I know all those years passed, I just can't picture it."

He was serious, his voice slowed with genuine regret. These were memories Blake couldn't latch on to, couldn't bring to life. He remembered the still frame photos of baby George that he'd studied in Iraq more than the experiences he'd been physically present for. It hit me: those were the years of chronic pain, years dulled by medication, years Blake lived like a ghost of himself.

I swallowed a reality that I had never allowed myself to confront. Addie, George, and I had, in many ways, lived those years without Blake. We lived beside him, establishing our own traditions—attending the Summit League basketball tournament each year, planning weekend getaways to the Great Wolf Lodge, at least one Minnesota Twins game each summer—carrying on like he wanted us to, needed us to, even. Like *we* needed to. Leaving Blake alone in sequestered silence. But I realized, too, that at the time, it was the best we could do, our way of making it through. All of this hit me, another impact of war, reverberating through our lives over a decade after Blake's homecoming. Seclusion and retreat. Survival, coping, moving forward. The realization magnified the significance of our connection there at the garden.

"So, I've been wondering about something," I said. "It's kind of coming out of nowhere." When I hesitated, Blake turned to face me, so I pushed ahead. "I've always meant to ask you. About Greg."

Blake nodded. His eyes shifted, not away from me, but from me to something else, something in front of me or beyond me, I couldn't tell. I fumbled. "I don't know why, and maybe I shouldn't ask, because you've never talked much about him, but I get the feeling it mattered to you a lot. *He* mattered to you." I paused, then filled uncomfortable silence with more words. "I guess it was Memorial Day that reminded me, but I've always wondered."

Blake sat a dripping Coors Light near his feet, shaking his head as he sighed, "Greg."

I thought about pulling back, telling Blake it was OK, that he didn't need to say anything, but the feeling returned that this was a conversation we needed to have. "You must have been closer to him. I mean, you knew him longer." I asked, "Is that why?"

Blake nodded slightly, pulling himself up from his lawn chair as he said, "Yeah, but it was more than that." He paced cracked cement. "Greg lived across the hall from me. With Grant."

Grant. I remembered our breakfast with him at the Reintegration Family Weekend weeks after their welcome home. I remembered running into him at a baseball game in Dell Rapids—how he told Blake they should get lunch sometime, and how surprised I was to learn that they did. Grant was the only soldier from Charlie Battery that I felt like I knew on any level, the only one Blake stayed in touch with. If Greg roomed with Grant, they must have all been friends. I imagined them packed into a small room in their tan, Army-issued T-shirts, trading *Simpsons* DVDs for seasons of *Family Guy* and *Seinfeld*. I imagined Greg as another Army buddy Blake would have stayed in touch with. If he were alive. It was a terrible thought. But so was the thought that maybe Greg's death was what kept Blake in touch with Grant.

"It was just so unexpected," Blake said, "because things had been pretty quiet. When we lost the other guys, it was right away, so we hadn't had time to know what to expect. But then, Greg. I mean, we hadn't seen any action for months. Plus, we only had a few months left. Guys were counting down, you know. We were over the hump. You just didn't see it coming."

I wanted to tell Blake he didn't have to say more, but I also wanted him to know it was OK to talk. The story poured out of him. "And you know, poor Grant. It really messed him up." Blake froze. He lifted hands to hips, tensed his shoulders so that his elbows pinched together behind him. "After Greg died, they came and told us, but then, usually they'd come clean out his stuff, like from his room. But they didn't. I don't know if it was because we were sort of close to going home, or what, but they just left it there. It ends up being months, and Grant has to live in that room with all of Greg's stuff. I mean, can you imagine? Weren't they supposed to send that stuff to his family?" He shook his head. "Maybe they did. I don't know, maybe that's not how it happened, but it just seemed like, I don't know. I just know Grant wasn't the same after that." He exhaled.

I apologized. "I'm sorry. Maybe I shouldn't have asked." I set down my beer.

"Yeah, no," Blake said, walking to the wide back door of the barn. "It's OK. I mean, I think about it too." I joined him, so that we stood side by side, facing north, staring out at the garden with its soil still freshly tilled from planting. We settled in to a heavy, but not unhealthy silence.

Finally, Blake asked, "Do you wanna hear something kind of bad?"

"I think so," I said cautiously.

"So, when you're done—when you get sent home—you usually leave your stuff for the next guys." I nodded to show I was following along. "TVs, bootleg DVDs, that kind of stuff." I waited for the bad part. Blake paced. "Well, I didn't leave any of it. For the next guys, I mean. I gave it to our interpreter."

I laughed. "That doesn't sound bad." I rubbed my hand, just briefly, on the small of Blake's back, remembering a string of wooden prayer beads he'd brought home with him, his explanation that his interpreter gave them to him. "That sounds like a really nice thing to do."

"It's just . . . " Blake squinted, as if trying to see something out of focus. "It's just like, the whole time you're following protocol, trying to do what you're supposed to do, but then none of it makes sense, so you just do what feels right."

"You just do the best you can," I said.

Blake nodded. "I guess so. You just start to wonder what difference it makes."

Settling back into silence, I studied the garden, its staked rows just starting to fill with green sprouts. I felt grateful. For Blake. His presence. This communication. I remembered a conversation I had with my uncle at a baseball game a week or so earlier. It seemed relevant, somehow, like the flip side of a coin. Greg Wagner's life was a promise, unfulfilled. But if we interpreted his death as a lesson in futility, we would lose our own opportunities for fulfillment, like this one. So, I said, "You know, I was talking with my uncle Al the other day, about family stuff—Grandma Betty, and your grandparents, and everybody—and it got me thinking about us. About moving back here. About the kids, growing up with their cousins. About the gardening, the Sunday dinners."

I leaned into Blake. "I was remembering when I moved home. I visited Grandma's grave, and I realized I wanted a life like hers.

A simple life. Centered. A family life." The shelterbelt that cut across the field in front of us shuddered in the breeze. "You know, you just follow where life leads you, and then you end up here. Like I told Al, I think I got what I wished for."

TWO YEARS LATER, after fourteen years of marriage, we received word that the Anderson family was ready to sell Marilyn's farm. This was Blake's dream, but it had become mine too. Ten acres of land, five outbuildings, room to spread our roots. When Blake told me the news, he seemed nervous. "So, are we really gonna do this?"

A laugh burst from my lips. "Are you kidding? All these years of dreaming, and now you ask? Of course, we are." I reassured Blake the same way I did our kids before sporting events or musical performances, reminding him that nervous and excited are two sides of the same coin, both reactions to uncertainty, both promises of possibility. "As long as we can afford it, why wouldn't we? It's your dream. You don't give up on it now when it's right there in front of you."

"I know," he said, toeing the wood floor of our living room. "It's just that we were making plans to do all that work on this house. I thought we'd decided we were just gonna stay here."

"Yes, but the contractor hasn't even come to give us a bid." I raised my eyebrows. "Serendipity."

Blake's eyebrows lifted into sharp peaks; dimples cut into his cheeks. "That is true."

"Of course, it's true." I leaned against a craftsman style built-in, suddenly realizing how much I'd miss this little house. But I felt ready to move on, too. "Call off the central air and refinished floors. Let's sell this place."

That weekend, we took the kids to the Anderson farm to show them around. When we pulled into the driveway, George scoped out where we could add a basketball hoop while Addie decided which barn would make the best chicken coop. I eyed the deck on the back of the house, thinking it just needed some stain, but no major work. We toured the house, claiming bedrooms and inspecting closet space. I proclaimed my love for the pristine, retro bathroom tile. "I seriously wouldn't change a thing in here. This bathroom is perfect."

"Except for the carpet," Blake pointed out.

"Well, yeah, the carpet," I agreed. "And I guess I'd take down the wallpaper and paint the walls white, to blend with the tile."

"You wouldn't keep that, would you?" George pointed to a cracked oak toilet seat.

"Yeah, probably not that either," I admitted. "But everything else—the ceramic tub, the matching toilet and sink, the tile—that stuff is perfect."

Addie chimed in, "And we're definitely keeping the corner toilet in the other bathroom, right? That's Uncle Brad's favorite." Obviously, there had been a lot of dreaming.

Blake raised his eyebrows in my direction. "What do you think?"

Of course, he was asking the larger question. What did I think about buying the place? But I answered, "Keep the corner toilet. Definitely."

The paperwork wouldn't happen for months, but when the time came, Blake showed me the letter of offer before sending it. "Just make sure it sounds OK. Make sure I haven't missed anything. I want it to be just right."

As a letter of offer on a home, I wasn't sure that it mattered much, but I took the printed page that Blake unfolded from the pocket of his dress pants, giving him a sideways glance that said, *I don't know why you're making such a big deal of this*. But when I read

Blake's description of how grateful he was just to have the opportunity to purchase the Anderson farm, to dream about adding an apple orchard on the ten acres, to spend the rest of our lives there, I understood that it wasn't formality he was worried about. He wanted Marilyn and her kids to understand that their home—the place where Dean and Marilyn lived their entire married lives—would be in good hands. It was emotional, not logical. It wasn't just another move or a financial investment. It was an investment in legacy—in their past and in our future.

We officially took ownership just after the New Year, but the house needed work before we could settle in. We tore out carpet and the half-finished basement that had absorbed moisture from the previous wet spring and a water leak the year before. We hired contractors to reinforce trusses so that we could tear out the wall that separated the kitchen from the dining and living rooms. When the time came to swing sledgehammers, Blake marveled at the construction of the sixties ranch—studs, covered in sheetrock, then wire mesh and plaster. "This place is built like a bomb shelter. It could withstand a nuclear fallout."

The overkill made remodeling especially tedious but gave us confidence in the solid structure of our new home. The process of painting walls, patching new oak floors to meet the old, then sanding and staining it all to match invested us in the work of perfecting what would be our forever home. We took pride in the work and the satisfaction of falling into bed on the mattresses we laid on bare floors, exhausted each night.

Our first home together had been a temporary honeymoon suite, where we'd lived as squatters, our future uncertain. Our second was the apartment we had tearfully rented, knowing we would never live in it together. Our duplex in Brookings was our first family home, our first taste of life together, but still transitional with Brock living in our basement, no sense of ownership. While Dell Rapids offered us the possibility of permanence, and we had made the home our own and lived happily there, it was also home to chronic pain, depression, and addiction—that fog of life we had lived through. De Smet had felt transitional, too, even though we loved our brick craftsman, loved each other and our lives there. It was a steppingstone. We knew we would outgrow it, eventually. As we embraced the task of remodeling, we embraced a new sense of purpose. This was the beginning of our happy ending—our forever, finally.

We placed weekly orders at our local home improvement stores, collecting tools and supplies as Blake became the handyman he had never been, and we tackled projects and the problems that came with them as a team, painting and installing baseboards and trim, plus staining and installing new kitchen cupboards. Blake studied hours of YouTube tutorials on the pouring of concrete countertops, building the confidence to take on the project himself. Blake was present in ways he had never been before. He fell in love with spray paint, sprucing up old door hinges and air vents with metallic paint, which we realized upon installation had an aluminum, space-age feel. Blake said, "It's like what someone in the sixties would have imagined the future would be like."

As pieces fell into place, I deemed our style mid-century modern farmhouse. We balanced modern stainless-steel appliances with the warm wood of cupboards and floors, a white shiplap accent wall, cool grey walls with a splash of color from the retro, paisley wallpaper in the entry that Blake insisted we preserve to date the house. One day the coincidental placement of an orange on the built-in shelf we'd painted white to match the new trim inspired me to add more splashes of yellow and orange in the form of throw pillows and sprigs of fake orange blossoms in a vase on the kitchen's floating shelves. While shopping for living room furniture I fell in love with what became known as the "space chair," grey leather perched on a curved chrome frame, a matching ottoman. I imagined the narrative. "We're like a sixties, space-race family. You work during the week at NASA, but we have this house in the country as our escape."

One day I hung a wooden gray sign on the wall with imprinted leather reading, "Be present, live simply, try new things. Choose joy, show gratitude, give generously. Love your life." Blake hated it. He said it had too many lines, the off-center spacing of words bothered him, and the sayings were all too cliché.

I brushed off Blake's commentary, thinking he couldn't be serious. He'd never cared about home décor before. He emailed from work the next day, explaining that when he said he hated the sign, he meant he *hated* it. He thought the wall space would be much better filled with the picture frame fashioned from antique tin ceiling tiles that I'd filled with smiling photos of our kids. He wanted décor that brought him joy. I defended the piece from a design perspective: the lines echoed the texture of the ship lap, but contrasted, since the wood was grey; the leather tied in the leather bar stools at our kitchen island; the clichés were actually meaningful to me, and if we lived by them, we would all be happier and healthier; the typescript was a nod to my love of words and writing. I thought the topic was still up for discussion and assumed we would revisit it later, so when the clouds parted that afternoon, I went for a run.

When I returned, sweaty and thankful for an hour to myself and refreshed by exercise, I expected to find Blake pleased with the fact that I'd swept and shined the floors he'd spent so many hours refinishing and the fact that I'd sorted through some of the relics the Andersons had left behind in the basement, which he'd been working hard to organize. I found him downstairs, working, but not at all happy. He deflected my small talk, and when I finally confronted him, asking him what was wrong, he blurted, "I come home from work, and the first thing I see when I walk in the house is that damn sign. I thought we agreed it was going to come down." I was speechless. What I thought was a non-emergency, a compromise-in-progress, was to him a direct insult.

We avoided each other most of the evening, and my frustration built. Finally, in a fit of rage, I took down the sign. But I also took down every decoration I'd hung, every picture I'd carefully placed. I knew it was an overreaction. As I stuffed pillows and blankets into garbage bags, I muttered to myself, "Fine, I guess we can't have anything I like, anything pretty or comfortable or meaningful in our house." When I began hauling bags and boxes across the yard to the granary, my strides lengthened with each trip, pounding anger out on the grass beneath my feet. Intoxicated by action, I hid everything away—four barstools included—in a storage room, simultaneously satisfied with and disquieted by my passive aggression.

When we revisited the conversation, things grew heated when Blake said, "Sometimes you act like you're the only the adult in the room, Amber, and you're not. My opinions matter too."

The comment stung. My response had teeth too. "You have to admit that for years, I was. For years, you were absent, spending every waking minute at work or hunting or baseball or the pheasant farm. We stayed out of your way, gave you space. I took care of everything, so it's kind of hard to get used to the fact that now you have an opinion on every single thing I do." Our conversation stalled again at that harsh reality, that remnant of so many years of side-by-side survival. He was right. So was I. This was a reality that we had circled, a bruise that we had avoided touching.

Our marriage had started with separation. I paid bills, made housing decisions and decorated those spaces, created bedtime routines and connection. When Blake came home from Iraq, I didn't want to push any of that on him, didn't want to overwhelm him. I wanted to be *enough* but never *too much*. But that became our normal. Silence, space, and separation proved effective coping strategies through our miscarriage, through Blake's chronic pain, through depression. It's not that we hadn't learned, too, to break silence as we clung to each other for survival, but we still tended toward it. We hid in it, sometimes, avoiding conflict as Midwestern and military values taught us to, sucking it up, stuffing struggles and emotions down rather than bringing them to the surface. Now, the threat of life and death had dissipated. Now, as we came closer to knowing ourselves and closer to knowing each other, we faced the challenge of adaptation, learning to let go of the things merely worth fighting *about* so that we might cling to those worth fighting *for*.

So, when the kids were finally in bed, we tried again. Sitting in our bare living room, walls devoid of decoration, and the couch cold minus its pillows and throws, I explained, "I'm just trying to create a comfortable, beautiful space for our family, and I'm not used to having every move I make questioned." I reached my hand out to rest it on Blake's knee. "I'm glad that you are involved. It's good for all of us—the kids need you, and I need you—but I guess it's harder than I thought it would be. Life, I mean. Just when you think you've got something figured out, everything changes. And when I feel criticized more than appreciated, I guess, it's just too much."

Blake accepted my explanation, putting his arm around my shoulder. "I know I could have been more careful with my words." He squeezed my arm, adding, "And I do appreciate you."

I accepted his apology by leaning into him, resting my temple against his shoulder. "I've never been very good at asking for help," I said, offering my own apology. "I really do appreciate your input. It's just, sometimes I forget that I can ask for it. Or that I should." As I leaned into Blake, I felt the beat of his heart through his chest, remembered the security I felt as a child listening to my Grandpa Cliff's breathing. Wanting Blake to understand how much that physical connection and our communication meant to me, I added, "I really do think we make a good team. I appreciate how your attention to detail balances out my half-assed, get-shit-done, good-enough approach, which can be dangerous. But I need you to know that even when I fail, I'm trying." Blake nodded. "And we can't just assume that we understand each other or that we can read each other's minds. We need to communicate."

Blake kissed my temple. "I do need to work on communication."

I smiled. "Well, I know your email was an attempt. Sometimes it's hard to look someone in the eye and say something you know they don't want to hear."

Blake lifted his head, making awkward sideways eye contact as he explained, "But I did mean it. I don't know why, but that sign makes me physically ill." I rolled my eyes and shook my head in somewhat mock disgust, still slightly injured by his disdain for something I truly liked. "But I don't mind if you move it, just somewhere else, where it's not the first thing I see when I walk in the door, the last thing I see when I leave. It leaves a bad taste in my mouth." I held my tongue, realizing that he would simply never be able to relax happily in our living room as long as the sign hung on the wall. It wasn't worth it. I wanted him present in our family home and happy there. Blake offered, "You could hang it in the bathroom. Or in our bedroom."

I laughed. "So that you can go to bed every night angry?"

He shook his head, "I don't spend my waking hours in the bedroom. It's dark most of the time when we're in there. I'm sure I could handle it." I relaxed into him.

THE NEXT DAY, after Blake left for work, and after the kids had eaten breakfast, I went for a walk. Unlike the runs I tried to squeeze in a couple of times each week on the days I felt confident and strong, this time I was searching for strength.

If it had been a running day, I would have brought our chocolate lab, Pam, and we would have run south for a mile. Then, when the road diminished to a minimum maintenance path, we would make a choice: west, toward the farm where I grew up, past the fields I drove with Dad to check cows, past the hedges of chokecherry and lilac bushes surrounding our old house; or east, where the landscape was less familiar, with the exception of Dolph creek meandering through the fields I passed, but where when I turned back, I could see the bright red barns of our current home from four miles out and run toward that promise.

But this was a different kind of day. A hard one. A brooding one. A sort of search or quest. I headed north. The thin ribbon of gravel no longer surprised me, like it had fifteen years earlier. Now I knew that just over a mile ahead lay the Scandinavian cemetery. Now I knew that the farmhouse I would pass on the way was home to several children, a couple horses, and at least a dozen chickens, so I knew better than to bring Pam with me. I knew that this contemplative path would lead me to Grandma Betty's grave.

As I walked, I thought about the fight I'd had with Blake the day before. Replaying the scene in my mind, I cringed at the image of me storming across the yard. My childish outburst embarrassed me even more in hindsight. And yet, like the gravel that crunched beneath my feet, the memory of Blake's words grated on me. *You act like you're the only adult in the room.* I asked myself why those words hurt so much, admitted that the answer wasn't only in the past. It wasn't just that when Blake was suffering, I *was* the only adult in the room. Sometimes it still felt that way. Things were so much better. *We* were so much better. But sometimes I did still feel alone and underappreciated.

My thoughts shifted back to Grandma. I wondered, *Did she ever feel this way?* It was impossible to imagine Grandma demanding recognition for her duties as a mother or a wife. Her service seemed selfless. Her baking and quilting and gardening seemed joyful, but that didn't mean it was effortless. I wished that instead of walking towards Grandma's grave, I were pulling into her driveway. That instead of sifting through my memories of her I could speak the words and hear her answer. *Grandma, did you need this kind of reassurance? Did you and Grandpa ever fight over something as stupid as wall décor?* It struck me: I was so young when Grandpa Cliff died. I had no real memories of them together, no evidence of what might have caused conflict between them, or how they might have handled it.

When the cemetery trees came into sight, I lifted my eyes to the horizon, the bright blue sky dotted with clouds, billowing like puffs of smoke. The clouds reminded me of my other grandma, Grandma Evie, and a conversation we'd had.

It was a stilted conversation, one I almost regretted at the time. We were driving to the hospital to see Grandpa Baine—it had to have been in the final months before he died—when I asked her about Grandpa Dayton. I realized that it was terrible of me to mention the loss of her first husband as she approached the near-certain loss of the second, but by that time, we had begun to realize how quickly we were losing her, too. Doctors had linked her memory loss to what they described as multiple mini strokes that she had been experiencing, unbeknownst to us, for years. I feared that if I didn't ask her about Grandpa Dayton soon, the opportunity would be gone forever. I had so many questions about him, about what life was like for the family after he died. After Blake's going to and returning from war, our stories had crisscrossed, and I'd felt that I needed her stories in order to make sense of my own. And so, I'd asked, "Grandma, how did you meet Grandpa Dayton?"

At first, she merely fidgeted beside me, sliding the fingers of one blue-streaked hand over the thin, waxy skin of the other. She looked out the window, pressed her lips together, and sighed. Looking down at her lap, she fidgeted with her bracelets and said, "You know, I guess I don't remember." Then, she lifted her left hand and tucked her thumb under to spin her gold wedding band, twisting until the diamond stood at center. Studying the square-set gem, she said, "It's awful, all the things you wish you could remember, wish you could understand, but you just can't."

As I turned back to the ribbon of highway ahead, I realized I had only seen one wedding ring on Grandma's hand, which didn't make sense. As a child, I loved to ask Grandma why she wore two diamonds, even though I knew the answer: "Because even after I married your Grandpa Baine I never stopped loving Dayton. He was my first love. Your mom's daddy." I began to question the accuracy of what I saw and what I remembered, but then Grandma spoke again, this time amazed, like a child. "Look at those clouds, so big and white against such a perfect blue sky. I wonder if I've ever seen any so beautiful in my life."

I told Grandma I had and proceeded to describe to her my wedding day, the photos of Blake and I against that same beautiful sky. I wondered if Grandma even remembered that I was married, or who Blake was, but she seemed to be following the conversation, so when another memory surfaced, I continued. "I remember those clouds from another day, too," I said. "The day Blake left for Iraq. When I hugged him goodbye, this is what I saw over his shoulder, this beautiful blue and white. It's silly I'd remember that . . . I don't know why . . . "

Grandma lowered her head, studying her wedding ring again. She spun it around her finger and said, "Those were hard days. That's why we remember them. Why we can't forget."

That conversation with Grandma Evie rushed back to me as I made my way towards Grandma Betty's grave. Although it wasn't unusual for me to feel the presence of these two women—I felt Grandma Evie's influence each time I baked a chocolate sheet cake or canned sauerkraut, Grandma Betty's when I made lefse or apple crisp—this felt different. I often remembered them in those idealized ways. Their perfect food. The warm memory of sleepovers with cousins. The soft focus of old Polaroid photos. Their presence, in those ways, felt like an inspiration but also a standard to try to live up to. This was more visceral, more immediate. This feeling was as quiet and comforting as a heartbeat.

I'd felt something similar before. One Sunday, as I played the closing hymn at church and sang along, "I will seek your loving will to guide me, o'er the paths I struggle day by day," I felt Grandma Betty's presence. The feeling rushed over me, a wave of emotion so strong that tears flooded my eyes, and I felt certain that if I turned toward the narthex, I would see her there in a belted dress and thick-soled shoes. I wanted so badly to turn, to study her long neck and square shoulders, her sharp nose. If I could turn my head just enough, maybe I could catch the whisper of words of the hymn slipping from her thin lips, but the notes and lyrics on the page before me demanded my attention. "Savior help me bear life's pain and sorrow till in glory I behold your face." I couldn't visually confirm Grandma's presence, but I felt it. My breath caught in my chest at the feeling of being enveloped by her.

With the gate leading into the Scandinavian cemetery now in sight, gleaming slightly in the shade of evergreens, I paused to examine the memories of my grandmas. Their lives had not been easy. They had both lost their husbands, witnessed their children and grandchildren's struggles, and suffered their own medical and no doubt emotional challenges. Their lives were not models of simplicity or perfection. They were models of perseverance and love.

Restored by this realization, I placed my hands on the silver gate in front of me, but rather than lifting the silver latch that would let me into the cemetery, I let the fence and the memories of these unwavering, gentle women support me. Knowing I had work to do, and now feeling strong enough to do that work, I turned toward home, but as I did, I smiled and nodded in Grandma Betty's direction, thinking, "You were right, Grandma. Those Jensen boys really are nice boys."

I didn't run home, but I walked lighter now, thinking no longer of the fight, but the resolution: my head on Blake's chest in our quiet living room, the rise and fall of his breath, the knowledge that at our best, we balanced out each other's strengths and weaknesses. We made a good team.

Once inside our single-story ranch, I peeled away the Command Strips I'd used to hang the sign Blake so hated. I couldn't help but laugh at the joy Blake would get from knowing that the sign left no permanent scars on the wall—Command Strips and pristine plaster were on the list of his new obsessions in our new house. In its place, I hung the large two-foot-by-four-foot frame, displaying photos of George and Addie at eight and four years old, respectively, and one of them hugging their chubby cheeks together as Addie squinted a cheesy smile. My first attempt placed the top of the frame awkwardly at eye level, the bottom hovering too close to the ground. Six inches made all the difference, and the first nail holes were concealed behind the frame. The hidden damage would be my little secret, my quiet defiance, the scars of miscommunication; the fact that every visitor to our home would comment on how perfect those photos were displayed in just that place, would be Blake's visible triumph. All of it would serve as a reminder of the importance of compromise, and a reminder that where there is smoke, there is potential for fire. Fire can be warm and comforting, life-sustaining, regenerating, even. But a smoldering fire, left unattended, can ignite and burn even the most secure structures down.

Our communication was still far from perfect, but after years of retreating, working independently side by side, we were learning to read each other's signals, to confront and concede, and to seek shelter together rather than to hide.

Blake and Amber on their wedding day, May 28, 2005.

Blake (front row, second from left) while serving in Iraq, 2005.

Amber's maternal grandfather,
Dayton Tarum.

Blake, Amber, and George at the welcome home for Charlie Battery, 1st Batallion, 147th Field Artillery unit on Sept. 30, 2006.

Blake and George in their Bryant Bucs uniforms, 2008.

Blake, George, Addie, and Amber in a family photo from 2010.

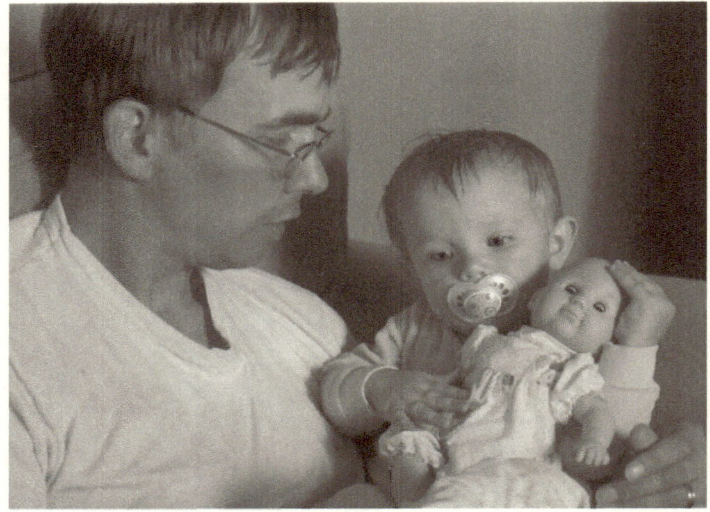

Blake and Addie, 2010.

Amber, George, Addie, and Blake in a family photo from 2013.

Amber with her maternal grandmother, Evelyn (left), and paternal grandmother, Betty (right).

Acknowledgments

Many thanks to my family full of storytellers and supporters, especially Blake, who encouraged me to make time to pursue my dreams, reminding me that if I waited for what seemed like the right time it would never come. To Christine and Mary, the teachers, mentors, friends, and midwives who encouraged me through the long labor of bringing this book into the world. To the friends and faculty of the University of New Orleans Low-Residency MFA program, especially Steven Church, who broke the news to me that I wasn't writing stories or essays but a book, and who warned me that the hardest part of writing it would be learning to claim time in the midst of motherhood and teaching to dedicate myself to the work. To Katey Shultz and the magical mountain experience of Pentaculum 2020 at Arrowmont School of Arts and Crafts, which offered me creative space to complete the most extensive revisions of the completed manuscript. To Tracy Crow for believing in the importance of a quiet story and the MilSpeak Foundation for championing the creative work of military veterans and their families—your tireless work is important and inspiring.

Photo by Addelyn Jensen

About The Author

Amber Jensen teaches courses in writing and literature at South Dakota State University in Brookings, South Dakota. Her work has been widely published in literary journals and anthologies to include *Oakwood, North Dakota Quarterly, O-Dark-Thirty,* and *Red, White, & True: Stories from Veterans and Families, WWII to Present. The Smoke of You* is her first book.

Thank you for supporting the creative works of veterans and military family members by purchasing this book. If you enjoyed your reading experience, we're certain you'll enjoy these other great reads.

American Delphi

by M.C. ARMSTRONG

During America's summer of plague and protest, fifteen-year-old Zora Box worries her pesky younger brother is a psychopath for sneaking out at night to hang with their suspicious new neighbor, Buck London, who's old enough to be their father. Their father, a combat veteran, is dead—suicide. Or so everyone thinks, until Buck sets Zora and her brother Zach straight, revealing their father as the genius inventor of a truth-telling, future-altering device called American Delphi.

Salmon in the Seine

by NORRIS COMER

One moment 18-year-old Norris Comer is throwing his high school graduation cap in the air and setting off for Alaska to earn money, and the next he's comforting a wounded commercial fisherman who's desperate for the mercy of a rescue helicopter. From landlubber to deckhand, Comer's harrowing adventures at sea and during a solo search in the Denali backcountry for wolves provide a transformative bridge from adolescence to adulthood.

Cry of the Heart

by RLYNN JOHNSON

After law school, a group of women calling themselves the Alphas embark on diverse legal careers—Pauline joins the Army as a Judge Advocate. For twenty years, the Alphas gather for annual weekend retreats where the shenanigans and truth-telling will test and transform the bonds of sisterhood.

Collateral Damage
2nd edition

by KEVIN C. JONES

These stories live in the realworld psychedelics of warfare, poverty, love, hate, and just trying to get by. Jones's evocative language, the high stakes, and heartfelt characters create worlds of wonder and grace. The explosions, real and psychological, have a burning effect on the reader. Nothing here is easy, but so much is gained.

—ANTHONY SWOFFORD, author of *Jarhead: A Marine's Chronicle of the Gulf War and Other Battles*

Sub Wife

by SAMANTHA OTTO BROWN

A Navy wife's account of life within the super-secret sector of the submarine community, and of the support among spouses who often wait and worry through long stretches of silence from loved ones who are deeply submerged.

Beyond Their Limits of Longing

Edited by
JENNIFER ORTH-VEILLON, PhD

In America, WWI became overshadowed by WWII and Vietnam, further diluting the voices of poets, novelists, essayists, and scholars who unknowingly set a precedent for the sixty-two successive, and notable, war writers who appear in this collection to explore the complexity both of war's physical and mental horrors and of its historical significance in today's world in crises.

Falling Off Horses

by KAREN DONLEY-HAYES

A mutual love for horses unites two young women as teenagers who forge an undying friendship that will steady them after countless falls from horses, a roller coaster of love losses and triumphs, the emotional pitfalls of equestrian breeding and competing—and finally, through the heartbreaking diagnosis of a fatal illness.

The Fine Art of Camouflage

by LAUREN KAY JOHNSON

A young woman's coming-of-age in the military against a backdrop of war, viewed through her lens as an information operations officer who wrestles with the nature of truth in the stories we hear from the media and official sources and in the stories we tell about ourselves and our families.

www.ingramcontent.com/pod-product-compliance
Lightning Source LLC
Chambersburg PA
CBHW031021160726
47991CB00005B/1825